THE NEW GHANA

THE NEW GHANA

The Birth of a Nation

J. G. AMAMOO

Authors Choice Press
San Jose New York Lincoln Shanghai

The New Ghana
The Birth of a Nation

All Rights Reserved © 1958, 2000 by J. G. Amamoo

No part of this book may be reproduced or transmitted in any form or by any means, graphic, electronic, or mechanical, including photocopying, recording, taping, or by any information storage or retrieval system, without the permission in writing from the publisher.

Authors Choice Press
an imprint of iUniverse.com, Inc.

For information address:
iUniverse.com, Inc.
620 North 48th Street, Suite 201
Lincoln, NE 68504-3467
www.iuniverse.com

Originally published by Pan Books

ISBN: 0-595-14915-4

Printed in the United States of America

To
MY MOTHER

CONTENTS

CHAPTER		PAGE
	PREFACE	ix
I	THE BACKGROUND	1
II	THE GREAT 'FORTY-EIGHT'	9
III	ACCORDING TO PLAN	22
IV	THE TEST OF THE TIMES	28
V	THE OLD ORDER CHANGES	48
VI	NEW TASKS TACKLED	56
VII	THE FINAL STEP	71
VIII	DEADLOCK!	91
IX	FROM GOLD COAST TO GHANA	107
X	GHANA IS BORN	112
XI	AFTER MARCH 6TH—WHAT NEXT?	117
XII	PROBLEMS OF INDEPENDENCE	123
XIII	UNANSWERED QUESTIONS	134
	APPENDIX A	139
	APPENDIX B	141
	BIBLIOGRAPHY	143

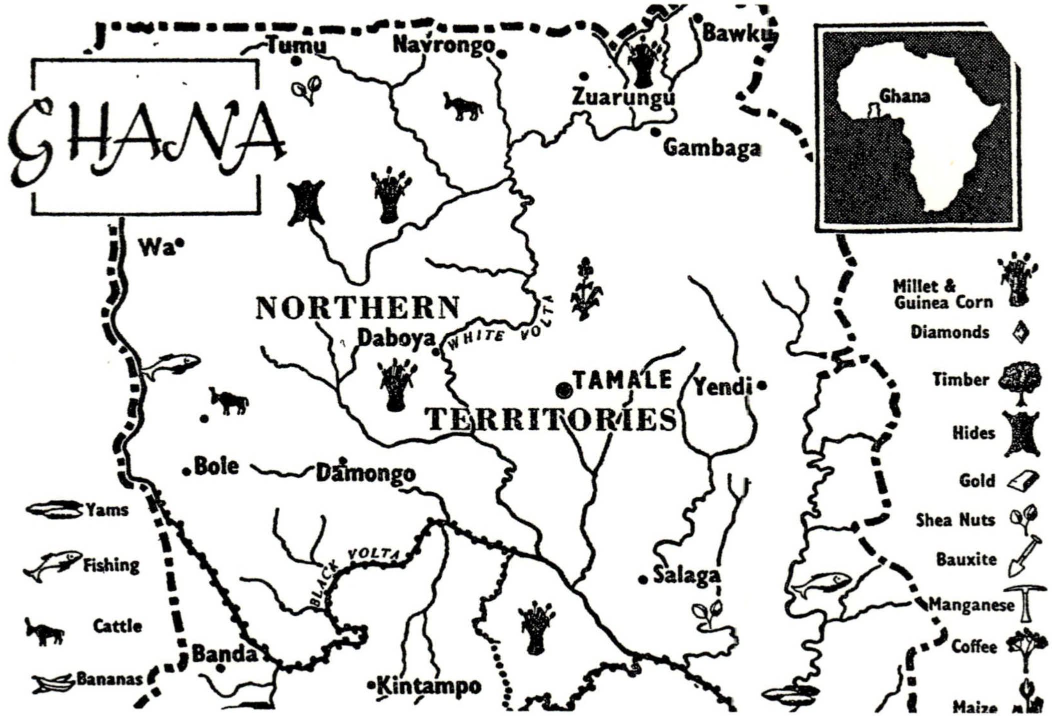
GHANA
Tumu
Navrongo
Zuarungu
Bawku
Gambaga
Ghana
Wa
NORTHERN
TERRITORIES
Daboya
WHITE VOLTA
TAMALE
Yendi
Bole
Damongo
BLACK VOLTA
Salaga
Banda
Kintampo
Yams
Fishing
Cattle
Bananas
Millet & Guinea Corn
Diamonds
Timber
Hides
Gold
Shea Nuts
Bauxite
Manganese
Coffee
Maize

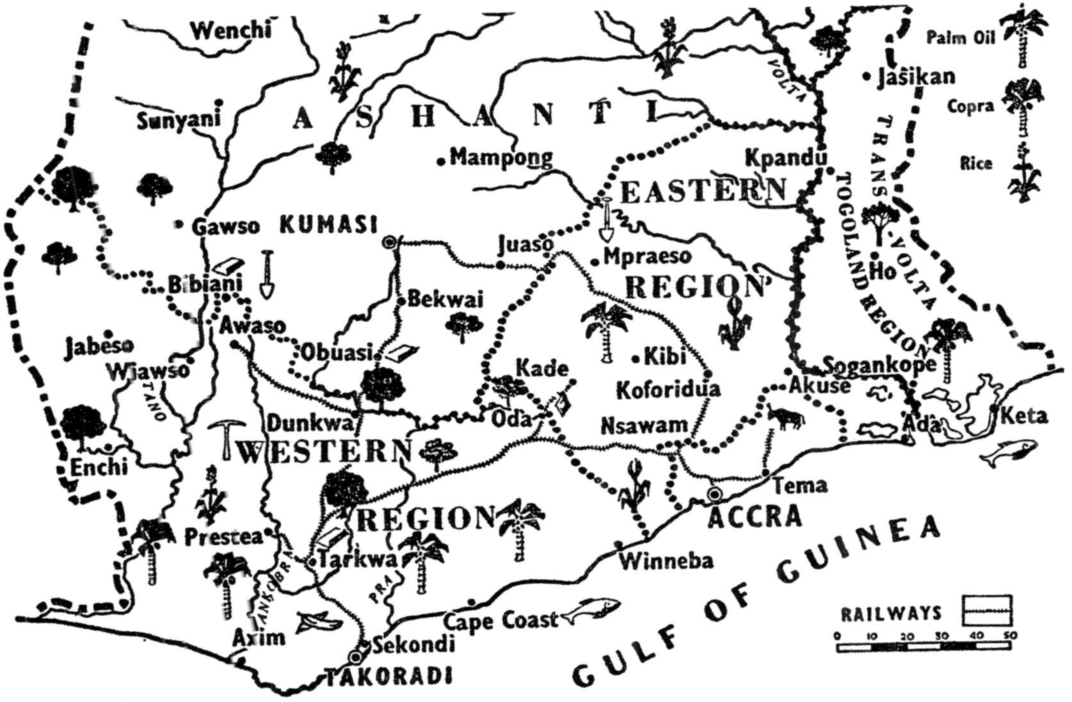

Wenchi
Sunyani
ASHANTI
Mampong
Gawso
KUMASI
Bibiani
Awaso
Jabeso
Wiawso
TANO
Enchi
Bekwai
Obuasi
Juaso
Mpraeso
EASTERN
REGION
Kibi
Kade
Koforidua
Oda
Nsawam
Dunkwa
WESTERN
REGION
Prestea
Tarkwa
ANKOBRA
PRA
Axim
Sekondi
TAKORADI
Cape Coast
Winneba
ACCRA
Tema
Akuse
Sogankope
Ada
Keta
Kpandu
VOLTA
Jasikan
Ho
TRANS-VOLTA
TOGOLAND REGION
Palm Oil
Copra
Rice
RAILWAYS
0 10 20 30 40 50
GULF OF GUINEA

The map on pages vi and vii
is reproduced by permission of
Educational Productions Ltd.
17 Denbigh Street, London, S.W.1

PREFACE

MY AIM in writing this book is to tell the human story of the evolution of the Gold Coast from a former British Colony in West Africa to the independent state of Ghana. The book does not claim in any way to be a textbook, nor does it even claim to be an exhaustive study of the period. All I have attempted to do in *The New Ghana* is to describe as fully as possible the chief constitutional and political events of the decade 1947–57 and the problems which now face the country. Consequently, I have purposely left out those incidents or events which, although they caused some political stir and comment in the country, do not to my mind have any political or constitutional significance.

The difficulties which beset any person attempting to write about contemporary events in Ghana are considerable, but I have tried to be objective and appeal as much to the head as to the heart. It is impossible to prevent party politics from creeping into a book of this nature, but where possible I have endeavoured to keep this tendency firmly in check.

The book is not designed to be an apology for any particular political party, but I feel strongly that most of the comments and conclusions could hardly be otherwise, considering the known facts and events of the period. I would, however, suggest that as fresh facts and more intimate knowledge become available, these may to some extent alter the general expressions of opinion which the book presents. We must leave that to the future.

I have written *The New Ghana* because I firmly believe that there is a genuine need both within Ghana and outside for a brief summary of its constitutional background

PREFACE

and its economic and political future, for there is little doubt that what has happened lately and is happening now in the country will go a long way in determining the fate of other Colonial peoples in Africa. The world watched to see how Ghana achieved its independence, and is watching keenly to see what Ghana will do with its newly won liberty.

Apart from the literature cited in the bibliography, I must make mention of that excellent, recently published compendium of facts, figures and commentary on Ghana, prepared by the Information Department of the Royal Institute of International affairs: *Ghana, A Brief Political and Economic Survey*.

I have also profited much from frequent discussions with some of my friends and colleagues at Adisadel College, Cape Coast, who have unwittingly helped me to discard erroneous ideas and views! I must mention my deep gratitude to Mr. E. V. T. Engman, B.A., for kindly providing me with considerable literature on the Togoland Problem. My heartfelt thanks go to Mr. K. A. Owusu-Ansah, B.Sc., for his firm, unremitting criticisms and help in other directions. To my friend Mr. W. F. Christian, B.Sc., I owe my thanks for his general advice and for his efforts to extricate me from my difficulties over problems of Ghana's agriculture and economy. Mr. T. W. K. Anderson gave me invaluable help. To Mr. Ammishaddai Adu, B.Sc., Achimota School, my thanks for kindly allowing me access to his comprehensive manuscript on some aspects of African culture and civilisation.

Lastly, the book would never have appeared had it not been for the encouragement of Mr. C.S. Barnes, Mr. E.K. Adane and Mr. S. A. Mensah and for their invaluable assistance, advice and patience. Nor should I forget my great indebtedness to my friend and former tutor, Rev. Eric Pyle, M.A., now on the staff of Cheshunt College,

PREFACE

Cambridge, whose enthusiasm was an inspiration to me at all times in the writing of this book.

All these persons have helped me tremendously, and if the errors in this book are few, it is certainly due to their efforts and advice; if any still remain, I alone am responsible for them.

In conclusion, I must thank the publishers for their invaluable assistance.

J. G. AMAMOO.

Accra, July 1957.

I
THE BACKGROUND

SOME COUNTRIES owe their prosperity to their geographical position; some owe their wealth and strength to their industries; others owe their national livelihood to their agriculture. Situated on the West Coast of Africa is Ghana, which has an area slightly greater than that of Britain, though the country does not support even a tenth of the population of Britain. Roughly rectangular in shape, it is bordered on the south by a short, rugged coastline, on the west and east by French Dahomey and French Ivory Coast respectively and on the north by French Sudan. Gambia, Sierra Leone and Nigeria are her nearest British neighbours, whilst Liberia, the only African republic in Western Africa, is close to her.

This small, sunburnt country produces about a half of the world's cocoa from her rich green farms, situated chiefly in the south and in Ashanti; whilst from her eastern mountains are produced mineral wealth—bauxite, manganese, gold and diamonds. The thick forests in the central parts of the country, with their tall, magnificent and heavy trees, provide timber of type unequalled anywhere in the world. The splashing Volta River, the only river of any importance in the country, affords boundless hopes and possibilities for a great industry in aluminium and hydro-electric power. As it flows from the north of the country right down to the coast, watering the barren lands of the north on its course, the Volta River offers a challenge to the country; a challenge that must be met with keen foresight, cool and comprehensive planning, and ample money and manpower to tap its immense resources, if the country is not to live in poverty in the midst and sight of wealth. From the barren, sandy north pour out small but increasing quantities of maize, millet and poultry products; exquisite leather-work and heavy, sturdy horses and cows.

Politically, Ghana is divided into four regions. On the south is the Gold Coast, the 'Colony', inhabited by tribes which have had a long association with the British in particular and Europeans in general. Here the majority of the people are either fishermen or sturdy farmers, or, where both these avenues for employment are lacking, those with education throw themselves into the service of the Government or British industries; with the result that it is in the 'Colony' that we find the most sophisticated people. Their advantage in being the first to imbibe Western civilisation has paid them dividends. They occupy quite a number of places in the public service and in the British firms, being found in diverse situations, from junior clerks to general managers and from clerical assistants to permanent secretaries. The reason for this heavy influx into public service and British industries is due mainly to the fact that the south is, in comparison, less wealthy.

North of the Gold Coast is a wide, roughly rectangular region with heavy forests, fertile farmlands and flourishing British mining concerns. This is Ashanti. The Ashantis are possessed of great wealth, which has tended to make them more independent and self-confident; also they are enriched with a history, brilliant through its victories in wars. With so many avenues open to them for developing themselves and making decent livelihoods, it is no wonder that extremely few Ashantis have found the Civil Service or foreign businesses desirable vocations.

As we go farther north, the thick green forests gradually merge into the thin grasslands of the Northern Territories, the most undeveloped region in the country where

THE BACKGROUND

the tough, tall, sturdy inhabitants occupy themselves chiefly with farming and the rearing of cows, sheep and horses. Here we meet the best horsemen, the most valiant soldiers and the most reliable yet simple people. Year after year, lack of jobs at home and the barrenness of their land force these finest of men on great treks southwards in search of a livelihood.

These three regions—the one-time 'Colony', Ashanti and the Northern Territories—constitute Ghana proper. However, a fourth region, Togoland, a long strip of land bordering the eastern side of the country, is also now incorporated in the country. Togoland, a perpetual problem to local nationalists, the British and the French, is inhabited by people who have a remarkable natural love for music due partly to their mountainous environment and partly to their association before the First World War with the Germans. Most of the great musicians in the country are the sons of Togoland.

This, then, is Ghana, a country of five million people, who despite national vicissitudes are proud and confident of a new era—a country now taking its seat as a responsible member in the comity of nations.

With British help, for example that of the United Africa Company, the country is developing very rapidly. The railway is only about six hundred miles long, connecting chiefly the mining centres and the important towns, but there are plans afoot for its development and extension. Apart from the only deep-water, modern harbour at Takoradi, there are no harbours or ports of any great commercial value in the country, but a very big harbour is now under construction at Tema. The improvement of ports already in existence is in view. The motor-roads still afford the most widespread means of travel. A few are bad but the rest are adequate, and if the improvement of the roads has not been very seriously tackled, it is due more to the fact that other projects are making priority claims on the finances of the country than to any negligence or incompetence on the part of the Government.

In the field of education great advances have been achieved. The country has its own University College, which is staffed by Europeans and Africans. Many secondary schools and training colleges are being built, whilst primary education is now almost free. Gradually a new generation is in the making, and it consists of boys and girls who are no longer fettered with the shackles of ignorance and frustration, which had been the lot of their fathers and grandfathers.

Yes, there are changes, rapid changes in all spheres of life. Under an amended law, qualified Continental and American doctors can now practise, thus alleviating the dire shortage of doctors in the country, and coupled with this move is the new scheme of training many Ghana doctors by awarding scholarships to deserving students.

Such, briefly, is the record of achievement in the last five years. It is an achievement by a black people—determined, imaginative, hopeful and confident.

The people of Ghana are of heterogeneous association who came originally from the Sudan—from those old, decadent and extinct Negro empires which once flourished in Western Sudan in the continent of Africa. The first recorded visit of Europeans was in the latter part of the fifteenth century, when the Portuguese began trading with the coast; two centuries later the British had also started trading. Their jurisdiction and powers were confined to the leases of lands they had obtained from the chiefs, and on these pieces of land they built forts and castles. Gradually the British extended the area of their jurisdiction by the acquisition of castles and forts from other European nations, chiefly the Danes and the Dutch, who were gradually losing their flourishing trade as the inhabitants became more aware that the British, apart

THE BACKGROUND

from being fair traders, were good soldiers and could be firm friends. The British traders as a result grew more influential and popular at the expense of the Dutch and the Danes.

Still there was no legal connection between the two countries—Britain and the Gold Coast; only a loose but rapidly developing form of friendship existed until, in 1844, certain Fanti chiefs negotiated a bond with the British. By the Bond of 1844 authority was given for the exercise of British jurisdiction. The chiefs were given British protection, and most of the obnoxious customs and practices of the people were made illegal. As the influence of the British grew, other states also associated themselves with the bond, so that by the end of the nineteenth century many chiefs had become connected with the British, and in 1906 the limits of the territories under British jurisdiction were clearly defined.

The British traders, having gained a strong hold on the coast, were anxious to maintain and expand their trade. This brought them into direct conflict with the Ashanti kingdom. A long series of wars ensued between the British and their native allies and the Ashantis until, in 1902, Ashanti was finally annexed as a British territory.

Little difficulty was experienced by the British in establishing themselves in the region north of Ashanti, where, anxious to extend their trade as widely as possible, they concluded treaties of friendship and protection with the native states. There were no wars, no misunderstandings. The Northern Territories became a Protectorate of Britain.

Without going into every detail of Ghana's history, it is worth noting here that it was only in 1874 that the Gold Coast was officially proclaimed a British Colony, and for the next seventy years British rule in the country ran smoothly, with the Executive Council, consisting of

British officers, and the Legislative Council, composed of an official majority and an unofficial minority of members, as the chief governing bodies.

From 1897 the British Government made progressive changes in the constitution of the country, but still the main governing body consisted of the Executive and Legislative Councils, both with official British majorities. With the establishment in 1925 of the Provincial Councils, which were bodies of state chiefs given statutory recognition by the British Government, a further advance was made in the constitution, with the result that the unofficial African members in the Legislature became almost as numerous as the official British members.

The establishment of the Provincial Councils undoubtedly served a great purpose in bringing the chiefs together, so that they could discuss freely their common problems and difficulties, but it also began the long, gradual process of estrangement between the chiefs and their subjects. The sessions of the councils necessitated the absence of the chiefs from their states for long periods, and, in addition, most people felt that the British officials exerted undue influence on the chiefs. In 1942 a further constitutional advance was made: two African unofficial members were added to the Executive Council, and the African membership of the Legislature was increased enormously.

All this time constitutionally the 'Colony', Ashanti and the Northern Territories had been separate entities; although from 1934 the Executive Council of the Gold Coast Colony was the Executive Council also of Ashanti and the Northern Territories. The Governor alone, however, put signature to their respective laws.

The greatest political advancement was made in 1946 with the introduction of a new constitution, popularly known as the 'Burns Constitution', after the Governor Sir Alan Burns in whose term of office it was introduced.

THE BACKGROUND

Undoubtedly it gave the country a considerable measure of self-government which it had not known before, and it united the 'Colony' and Ashanti, and indirectly the Northern Territories, under a single Legislature. The two main features of this constitution were as follows. First, the Governor reserved his power of veto. Second, an African unofficial majority, partly nominated and partly elected, was established. Thus, for the first time in the history of the country the official British majority in the Legislature disappeared.

The country was now enjoying some good measure of responsible government. The new constitution was heartily welcomed by all sections of the people and the Press, and the British Government was praised for its magnanimity. Indeed, there was no one in the country who openly attacked or criticised this new form of government, and those who had taken part in drawing it up modestly praised themselves for their political acumen and the statesmanship they had shown. There was real understanding between the Government and the people, and there were hopes of a bright future. This fact must be very carefully borne in mind when considering the events of the next two or three years after the promulgation of the 'Burns Constitution'. Few in 1946 discovered any loopholes or anomalies.

The arrival in the country of Kwame Nkrumah, however, in the following year, 1947, was the signal for violent attacks on the 'Burns Constitution'. The trouble was that it had been drafted to suit conditions in 1943, and that the next three years had wrought vast changes in the opinions and ambitions of the people. The constitution was out of date. Changes must be made or revolution would result. Nevertheless, neither the British Government nor the Africans who had drafted the constitution envisaged overnight the vast changes which Nkrumah was to demand.

THE NEW GHANA

Kwame Nkrumah, after a varied education in America and Britain, arrived at the invitation of a newly formed political party, the United Gold Coast Convention, to be its Secretary. Before he came, a seasoned local politician, Dr. J. B. Danquah, had been steering its course. As soon as Nkrumah took on the job, Dr. Danquah's position began to weaken as the new Secretary became more powerful and popular.

A mass orator of great ability, the enviable possessor of a powerful personality and a man of academic brilliance, Nkrumah made extensive tours, popularising the Convention and enlisting more and more members. Other leaders of the new organisation toured different parts of the country, delivering their message of goodwill and political freedom. Everywhere the leaders went they received a rapturous welcome. It seemed that at long last a stable organisation had arisen to fight for self-government for the people. And in about eight months the masses had become so inflamed that a revolution appeared imminent.

II

THE GREAT 'FORTY-EIGHT'

THE YEAR 1948 was a great year in the history of Ghana for reasons unconnected either with the arrival of a new Governor or the first political tumult, with its loss of many lives and damage to property. It saw the beginning of so many tremendous changes, constitutional, economic and social, that it has become a pivot on which the modern history of Ghana has been rotating. Superficially, the disturbances of February–March 1948 were caused by the clash between the police and a few hundred unarmed ex-servicemen on parade in the capital town. A detailed study of the events shows that the whole people, as much as the Burma veterans, were the cause of the disturbances. The riots were the outburst of pent-up feelings and grievances, some of them generations old, against all aspects of the life of the body politic.

First, let us analyse the political causes of the upheaval of 'forty-eight'. For a long time most educated Africans who had a bent towards politics had been feeling that they could never have an opportunity of helping to shape the destiny of their country. All important appointments in the Government were held by British officers, who relied for support not on these politicians but on the chiefs, through whom indirectly the country was governed, and the suspicion had grown that the chiefs were in league with the British to stifle the political aspirations of the people. This suspicion alienated the British and brought the chiefs into great contempt and dislike. What the constitution of 1946 did was to confirm the fears and suspicions of people that, so long as the chiefs took an active part in politics, they would always be an impediment to rapid political advance.

The granting of self-government to India and Burma in 1947 and 1948 had a tremendous effect on some of the politicians in the country. They felt that now was the chance for them to speak, or for ever hold their peace. There were, therefore, constant references to India and Burma in political lectures and rallies, organised by the political organisations. Most of the soldiers who had served overseas on returning home felt that the promises which were given them before their enlistment were not being fulfilled. Their feeling for national consciousness was also developing, due in the main to contacts with men of other nationalities during their stay overseas.

The ex-servicemen had genuine grievances. They felt that their disablement allowances and other allowances due them were too scanty and not in proportion to the rising cost of living. They felt that they were not being rehabilitated and resettled quickly enough. In short, they felt that they had been misled and ill-treated. These ex-servicemen were to be found throughout the country, even in the remotest villages; wherever they were, dissatisfaction reigned.

Most people, especially the local traders, were highly incensed at the increasing prosperity of foreigners, particularly the Syrians and Lebanese. The rate of prosperity of foreign traders appeared to be in inverse proportion to their own, and they began to attribute all their troubles to this fact. The result was a hostile front to the majority of non-Africans.

Finally, there was the perpetual suspicion that the Government, although paying lip-service to the policy of 'Africanisation', was dead against it. The educated class, especially those in the Civil Service, felt that the Government, despite constant assurances to the contrary, did not like appointing Africans to posts in the senior service.

THE GREAT 'FORTY-EIGHT'

Africans who had been in the junior service for a long time, some for as many as twenty or twenty-five years, and were hoping for promotion, were disappointed on being told that although they had the necessary experience they lacked the prerequisite qualifications. Even graduates, with the required qualifications, were told, more often than not, that they were ineligible. It was a paradoxical situation, and a sense of frustration gradually led to a feeling of contempt for the Government and a hatred of the expatriate British officers. According to official figures, in April 1948 there were between 1300 and 1400 senior appointments in the Gold Coast Administration. Of these 98 were held by Africans, i.e. about 8 per cent at most, and the rest by British expatriate officers. The problem of the recruitment and employment of European staff is at all times a delicate one, which requires fair and honest handling. Suffice to say here that it was a sore problem to the whole country in 1948.

The economic causes of unrest were diverse: the acute shortage of goods following the end of the war and the consequent enormous rise in prices; the alleged unfair distribution of goods in short supply; the continuance of wartime controls on commodities; a growing doubt of the Government's interest in the development of the country. All these grievances, coupled with the Government's stated unconcern for the economic welfare of the people so far as their relations with foreign traders and firms were concerned, formed a fertile field for revolution. The shortage of goods and the rise in prices following the cessation of hostilities were natural and no more the fault of the Government than an epidemic or a typhoon; but the Gold Coast people felt that foreign traders were taking undue advantage to fleece them.

There was another issue which was a source of constant friction and anxiety. For some years the cocoa trees had been attacked by a certain virus disease, called Swollen Shoot, which was rapidly devastating the cocoa industry, upon which the whole economic foundation of the country depends. Scientists detailed by the Government to study the causes and remedy for the disease had come to the conclusion that only wholesale cutting-out of the diseased cocoa trees, followed by an intensive campaign of replanting, could save the industry from utter devastation and extinction. Naturally, the farmers did not easily swallow this decision. The Government passed a law enforcing compulsory cutting-out. This move brought forth spontaneous resistance from the farmers, who were prepared to stake all they possessed, even their lives, to preserve their trees. The result was that all over the country the Government and the councillors who had been connected directly with the law, fell into disfavour. So hostile had the farmers' attitude become, that by January 1948, just a year after its introduction, farmers were resorting to arms to defend their trees from the axes and cutlasses of the battalions of cutting-out officers.

However, these were not the only causes of the disturbances of '48. We must next consider the social causes of the riots. There was the question of education; although there was quite a number of primary schools in the country, facilities for higher education were so limited that very few ever enjoyed any secondary education, let alone the blessing of university training. For a people innately desirous of learning, the general educational facilities in the country were too few. There was, too, much unrest due to the gross disparities between the salaries of the natives and foreigners, the acute and deplorable housing conditions, especially in the towns, and unemployment, which was rife.

These, then, were the causes of the riots of '48. There were grievances, some of them generations old, nursed to maturity, so that all that was needed to set the whole

THE GREAT 'FORTY-EIGHT'

country ablaze was the application of a tiny spark to the gunpowder of social and economic dissatisfaction. The spark was produced jointly by a chief and a body of ex-servicemen, and the flames were fanned by the oratory of Kwame Nkrumah.

By the end of 1947 the cost of living had risen so much and the prices of imported goods had become so high that the chiefs felt something must be done, and quickly at that, to ease the situation. Joint efforts by the chiefs to persuade the Administration to use its good offices to help reduce the rising cost of living met with cold reception from the Administration. Then a certain sub-chief of Accra, Nii Kwabena Bonne III, a man of considerable business acumen, organised a campaign to boycott European goods. He toured the country, explaining his plans to the chiefs and people. His idea was welcomed and accepted everywhere. The chiefs next gave their statutory support to Nii Kwabena Bonne's idea, and on January 25th, 1948, the boycott was put into effect. It was successful throughout its application, due in the main to its drastic enforcement by the native authorities. One would have thought that the European companies would have done all they could to prevent the imposition of the boycott; in fact, they allowed matters to go ahead with breakneck speed, convinced apparently that the Africans could never unite and carry out such a plan successfully.

It would seem that this illusion had permeated the Administration. There was general conviction that the Africans could never organise a strong, united front and that they were in such dire need of imported goods that they would very soon yield. Later events were to show how grossly incorrect had been British impressions about the character of the African. Below the apparent obsequiousness, the tribal differences and the mutual mistrust, there lay a fervent national consciousness which, properly aroused and directed, was capable of great feats. And it is unfortunate and tragic that there had to be so much wanton destruction of property, so much bloodshed, before many Europeans had learnt this lesson.

The boycott was so successful that on February 11th, 1948, the Government, which had earlier declared openly that it was a trade dispute between the people and the foreign traders, and was therefore not going to interfere in it, was forced to arrange a series of meetings between the Chamber of Commerce on the one side, and the Nii Bonne Committee and the chiefs on the other, with the Governor's deputy as chairman.

But the atmosphere was already over-charged with excitement and racial enmity. The boycott had started as an economic feud and was ending as a racial battle. Late in February of '48 it was announced by the Government on the radio that as a result of the negotiations which had been going on, there would be reductions in the prices of some imported goods, and that the boycott would be lifted on February 28th, 1948. The Africans felt that at long last prices were to be scaled down and things were going to be better. They felt that they had won a remarkable victory over the foreign companies, but they still doubted the faith and sincerity of the foreigners. And so in the morning and afternoon of that memorable February day, hundreds of people gathered in front of the large European-owned shops and stores in Accra, waiting to get in to find out whether prices really had been scaled down. Already the atmosphere had become so bitterly charged with racial feeling that it was quite evident that there would be some catastrophic incidents should the excited populace feel disappointment. When at last people did get into the shops they found that the reductions were much below their expectations and their anger knew no bounds.

As if by coincidence, the ex-servicemen in the capital, Accra, had obtained a permit to have a procession through

THE GREAT 'FORTY-EIGHT'

the town on that same day. Their original plan had been to present a petition direct to the Governor at his official residence—Christiansborg Castle; but it was finally agreed that they should send it to a senior official at the Secretariat, who would hand it over to the Governor at his residence. Accordingly, the petition was handed in at the Secretariat by the leaders of the ex-servicemen on the afternoon of February 28th, 1948, and the procession began on a route prescribed by the Commissioner of Police.

Naturally, there were a lot of civilian sympathisers in procession with the veterans. By three o'clock the procession had, after deviating from the official route, reached Christiansborg Crossroads, from which there was a road leading to Government House. At that point the unarmed procession came face to face with a small police detachment, under the command of a British officer, Superintendent C. H. Imray, who, fearing that an attempt might be made on the Governor's life and anxious to frustrate it, after due warning, opened fire on the crowd.

Confusion reigned. The crowd, highly inflamed and devoid of any weapons of defence or offence, resorted to stone-throwing, but stones were poor weapons against rifles and revolvers. To this incessant torrent of stones, the police detachment replied with more shooting. Within a short time there was a considerable number of casualties, and to a people not used to rioting or being shot at in public, this characteristic display of the effectiveness of British arms was worse than a massacre. For the first time in modern history, British arms had made themselves effectively felt against the African, and from that memorable day, February 28th, 1948, the political atmosphere in the country was unsettled till after the General Elections in February 1951.

As soon as the news of the shooting was flashed in Accra, the excited, infuriated masses, already feeling strongly that the Europeans had deceived them by not scaling down the prices enough, began to break through the shops and warehouses of British, European, Indian and Syrian firms. Looting of goods, especially imported goods, started, and pent-up wrath which the discontented masses had been nursing was vented on all foreigners. The houses of Syrians were broken into; cars of Britons and wealthy Africans were turned over and set on fire. There was pandemonium everywhere. All efforts by the police to control the situation were fruitless, and throughout the evening wanton destruction, both of life and property, went on. Soon the news had been flashed all over the country that riots had broken out in Accra. The fever of rioting was quickly caught by the chief towns and by some smaller towns. Looting, beating and shooting went on in all important towns for some three or four days before order could be restored by the military.

The Governor Sir Gerald Creasy, after some vacillation, faced the situation realistically. He proclaimed a state of emergency. The police detachments in all the towns were armed and reinforced. Barricades were erected in the streets of the capital, and lorries and cars were searched at definite points on the roads. An emergency police division was hurriedly created and trained to combat further looting and rioting. Censorship was imposed on the country. All these measures helped to mitigate the situation, but sporadic rioting still went on.

Then Sir Gerald Creasy, who incidentally had arrived in the country less than two months before the incidents, went a step further in his efforts to restore peace and tranquillity. On March 12th, 1948, he issued removal orders against Dr. J. B. Danquah, Kwame Nkrumah and four others, whom he believed were fomenting the troubles and were perhaps planning further disturbances. His action resulted in further outbreaks of rioting and strikes, and in the latter college students took part.

By the middle of March the situation was fully under

THE GREAT 'FORTY-EIGHT'

control. The Governor had to confess that he had been overtaken by events. The first disturbances in the 'model colony' were ended. More than twenty-nine people had died in the disturbances and more than 230 people had sustained severe injuries. Both classes of casualties were due partly to the shooting by the police and the military, and partly to the fights which had taken place between looters and looted.

Thus closed the darkest chapter in Ghana's history. From that day, February 28th, 1948, the Gold Coast ceased to be a 'model colony'.

A Commission of Enquiry, led by Mr. Aiken Watson, Q.C., and consisting of three eminent Englishmen, was appointed by the British Government in April, and it began sitting on April 9th, ending a month later. One cannot but be proud of the impartiality and fairness with which this commission did its work, showing favour to neither African nor European. It held public and informal sessions, visited the chief towns, and met as many different people as possible. When the Report of the Commission came out in the middle of the year, the whole country was pleased. They felt that they had been treated fairly. The Report criticised the Government's Africanisation policy, its lethargy in the economic sphere and its general weakness. It also recommended a host of political reforms, which were destined to grant the country a sizeable measure of autonomy. The Watson Report, so-called after the chairman of the commission, was just, despite the possible feelings of some nationalists. In fact, Mr. Kofi Baako, a young comrade of Kwame Nkrumah commenting on the report a year later, wrote, 'assessing the Report as a whole, one is bound to say that it is on the whole satisfactory'.[1]

The United Gold Coast Convention enjoyed its best days during the period prior to and following the sitting

[1] Kofi Baako in *Without Fear*.

of the Watson Commission. The cause of the six detained men was championed by Mr. Dingle Foot, a British barrister. All the accused men explained their political backgrounds and philosophies and digressed on the country's conditions, but the man whose hearing caused the greatest sensation was Kwame Nkrumah, who was accused by the Government of being a Communist.

Innumerable resolutions were sent by various organisations and associations to the commission all asking for full self-government; thousands upon thousands enrolled as members of the U.G.C.C., and its leaders at once became popular, national figures. Kwame Nkrumah enjoyed a similar position to John Wilkes in England in the eighteenth century. He drew crowds everywhere he went—and he went almost everywhere; lectured in the parks and in the markets and at waysides, and in the towns, villages and even in the sub-villages. He contacted all; talked to all; and tried to show people that everything depended upon their firmness.

By this time Nkrumah's paper, the *Accra Evening News*, had become a national organ, and it was normal to see queues in front of its office and hundreds of people poring over that single-sheeted paper. The editor was a Mr. K. A. Gbedemah, who cleverly put on paper the organisation's policy, programme and activities. The paper thus became the mouthpiece of the U.G.C.C. since the organisation had no organ of its own; but—and this must be noted well—it was Nkrumah's own paper.

The Watson Report was put before the Legislative Council for consideration, and after much deliberation the recommendations of the commission were accepted in principle. However, the report had recommended that a local committee, consisting of men who knew and understood well the country's condition, should be set up to draw up some form of solid constitutional recommenda-

THE GREAT 'FORTY-EIGHT'

tions; in other words, to advise on how best to implement the recommendations of the Watson Report.

It was over the choosing of that committee that emotions flared up once again. The nationalist papers, chiefly Nkrumah's paper, pleaded for an opportunity to be given to the masses to choose men of their own liking; and, uninterruptedly, this plea was widely publicised so that within a very short time it had grown into a national demand. The *Accra Evening News* challenged the right of the Government to nominate people to draw up a constitution for the country, and asked that the people should elect their own men in whom they had confidence.

The Government would not agree to this. It chose to nominate the men, and in December 1948 the list of the names of the members of the committee was issued.

This was a victory for British diplomacy, for the list included all African members of the Legislative Council, some staunch nationalists, including all the six detained men, except Nkrumah, and a substantial number of moderate elements. It was a fair deal, and the most rabid among the nationalists could find little fault with it. In fact, most of the men nominated by the Governor would have been elected by the people if they had had the chance; though, of course, there were certain men considered as reactionary who would never have found themselves on the committee.

Before the list was issued it was announced that the chairman of the committee would be an African judge, Mr. Justice Coussey. Nkrumah did not challenge the integrity of the judge, nor his good faith or eminence, but he challenged the utter disregard that the Government had shown of public opinion in nominating the chairman. And for some weeks the *Accra Evening News* kept on making the issue clear and direct to the masses.

Another source of controversy over the committee was the appointment of its secretaries. It was announced that it would have two secretaries, one an African administrative officer, Mr. A. L. Adu, a brilliant, highly respected and affable man, and the other a British administrative officer. Trouble started at once. Nkrumah attacked the Government for having chosen the secretaries, and, what was more, for having included, without authority, a European on a committee which was to be 'all-African'. It was strongly believed that the white secretary had been added for ulterior motives.

The fact that Nkrumah was the only man amongst 'The Six' to be excluded from serving on the committee was a bad mistake on the part of the British and produced an awkward situation, which has affected the country to this day. Whether it was fear or distrust which led them to exclude him, only future historians can tell. But, first of all, it allowed Nkrumah full scope to carry on his activities, while the other nationalists were busily serving on the committee. As a result, for some time only Nkrumah's voice was to be heard, and he certainly was not slow to utilise fully the great opportunity which had offered itself. Secondly, many people thought that Nkrumah had been left out because he was too strong for the British to handle, and was therefore too dangerous to be allowed on the committee, the other leaders being relatively mild or 'moderate' and therefore harmless. Thirdly, the fact that those who were on the committee were not elected by popular vote, but were nominated by the Government, went a long way to discredit the nationalist leaders who were on the committee. They were charged with having compromised with the British, and their report was rejected in advance.

Moreover, before the list of the members of the committee had been released, a significant event had taken place, and its result was to seal the doom of the committee's report in general. Late in 1948 the Government received an invitation to send delegates to the African

THE GREAT 'FORTY-EIGHT'

Conference to be held in London. The Government chose the delegates, some of them British officials, the rest Africans, and among these was Dr. J. B. Danquah. The *Accra Evening News*, and therefore the public—for what it said largely formed public opinion—told the Africans, and in particular Dr. J. B. Danquah, not to accept the invitation, but to stay at home and utilise their time and energy in constructive thinking and planning. Soon the majority of the people, especially in Accra, were advising the doctor not to attend the conference. They argued that as one of 'The Six' it would mean much if he went. It would mean compromise or something greater than that. But Dr. Danquah chose to go, and with the other members of the delegation he left port for London. At last the die was cast, and to crown it all reports from Mr. George Padmore, a well-known West Indian journalist, were to the effect that the doctor had spoken in compromising tones. He at once forfeited public confidence, and long before he returned the ground was very much prepared for a change.

Meanwhile, the U.G.C.C. leaders went on recruiting members and supporters in thousands, the vast majority owing unsworn allegiance to Kwame Nkrumah, about whom the country was to learn so much more in the next year and whose oratory, without doubt, had attracted these new members.

III

ACCORDING TO PLAN

IN JANUARY 1949 the Coussey Committee, so-called after its chairman Justice Coussey, started sitting *in camera*. At once the *Accra Evening News* organised committees which immediately began to send resolutions, asking the Coussey Committee to grant the country full self-government. A flood of letters and telegrams were received to the same effect, with an added plea for a legislature with two chambers.

It is impossible to understand the situation properly without following the activities of Nkrumah during this period. As secretary of the U.G.C.C. and as its star figure, he had organised the youth into a strong, solid unit; indeed, he paid much attention to the younger people. It may be that, being youthful himself, youth attracted him. Or it may be that the young men and women saw in him a man of similar blood; or it may be that he admired vigour and youth and action but was himself being denied freedom of movement. Whatever the reason, there grew up within the U.G.C.C. another body owing unsworn personal allegiance to Nkrumah. With the aid of other young nationalists, who presumably felt something slow about the activities of the U.G.C.C., he founded the Committee-on-Youth Organisation, popularly known as the C.Y.O., and became its first chairman, with, as its Secretary, an efficient, quiet, unassuming man, Mr. Kojo Botsio, of whom we shall hear later.

From the day of its formation in 1948, the C.Y.O. seemed to have taken on itself all the activities of the U.G.C.C., and it appeared as if they were one and the same. In December 1948 the C.Y.O. published a pamphlet, *The Ghana Youth Manifesto*, in which, among other things, it vehemently advocated immediate self-government, asked the Coussey Committee, then about to sit, to recommend it, and also outlined the policy it would adopt in self-governing Ghana; and it was not sheer accident that the pamphlet was dedicated to the United Gold Coast Convention. The C.Y.O. could not as yet have done otherwise; lectures and meetings continued to be called by the U.G.C.C., but under the auspices of the C.Y.O. A copy of the C.Y.O. resolution was printed in the *Accra Evening News* and agreed by all U.G.C.C. branches before it was forwarded to the Coussey Committee.

The years 1947 and 1948 were years of luck and prosperity for the U.G.C.C., but 1949 held a different message. Early in the year the political atmosphere began to darken. Feelings were running high, the Press continued to repeat 'self-government or nothing'; tension was increasing. Nkrumah was touring every part of the country telling the people to "Let the Coussey Committee realise that the country would not accept anything short of full self-government".

At this juncture a British legal expert, holding a high position in the Colonial Office, arrived on the scene. He had come to advise on sport. The whole country was at once infuriated by this apparent display of tactlessness. Everywhere that Sir Sydney Abrahams went to give talks on sport, he was booed and treated with scorn and antipathy. It was felt that once again British diplomacy was on the move. Some of the papers counselled for respect and tolerance, but the *Accra Evening News* directly attacked Sir Sydney's mission on the grounds that though they knew how beneficial sport could be to a self-governing nation, this was not the time to give talks on it. In fact, some of the headlines were SELF-GOVERNMENT, NOT SPORT, WE WANT S.G. Many people felt that his mission was calculated to draw them gradually and alluringly from their demand for self-government, and as such they refused to have anything to do with it. This feeling was heightened by frequent remarks of the leaders, especially Nkrumah, to that effect.

Sir Sydney Abrahams was invited to a mass meeting of the United Gold Coast Convention at Accra, and at last the bubble burst. The speeches were drowned in shouts of 'Self-government, not sport'! 'We demand self-government now', and the meeting ended in pandemonium. The papers criticised Dr. Danquah first for having invited a British official to a national political meeting, and next for allowing sport to be the subject at a political meeting. Danquah tried to explain his actions, but already confidence in him had been weakened. Yet whilst apologising to the late Sir Sydney Abrahams for the gross misconduct shown to him during his visit, and whilst being sincerely sympathetic to him for the utter frustration which he can but have felt, it must be argued that his mission was remarkably ill-timed. For this the blame goes to those who invited him; particularly, to those among them who were in the country and must have known how high feelings were running. No one challenges Sir Sydney's athletic prowess—he was an Olympic athlete in his youth; but this was not the moment for his visit. Nkrumah saw the subtle advantage to be gained, and made the best use of it—to discredit the mission and the British.

Signs of a split in the national front were now becoming discernible, and matters which had been the secret of the conference room were becoming public. There were hints that a rift had developed between Nkrumah and the rest of the leaders of the U.G.C.C. Also rumour had it that he had been, or was going to be, removed from his post as secretary and made financial secretary—a rumour which most people wishfully refused to believe. Finally, it had become common knowledge that the C.Y.O. was to be dissolved, and the youth were prepared to move heaven and earth to foil this plan.

Negotiations were going on among the U.G.C.C. leaders, when the Annual Easter Conference of the organisation took place at Saltpond, the birthplace of the U.G.C.C. The delegates had to make final decisions on many issues, and this was no time for vacillation. The present generation are not in a position to assess fully the value to the country of the deliberations at that conference. That must be left to posterity. But we can state that it was a protracted conference, which was attended by all the delegates. There was much havering and indecision, and instead of thrashing out the differences between the two camps of thought, symbolised by Nkrumah and Danquah, the situation was merely aggravated and no cogent decisions appeared likely to emerge from the conference. Events were drawing to a climax.

One day, after a hectic session, emotions reached boiling-point. On that memorable day the atmosphere was excessively charged. The crowd outside the conference hall waited anxiously for details of the proceedings. Nkrumah came out of the hall and in a grave but short speech informed the crowd that the C.Y.O. would be dissolved; that he had now realised that his very life was in danger. The crowd sighed, and at once asked him to resign and said they would follow him till death. He questioned their sincerity. They promised their everlasting support. They emphasised again that he must resign or join the 'moderates'. He again tested their confidence in him. The result was reassuring. There and then the letter of resignation was written and signed. Nkrumah returned to the conference and read his paper of resignation. The sad faces were now all smiles. Nkrumah no more held an executive post in the U.G.C.C. though he continued to be an ordinary member until his resignation in August, 1949.

There followed a pitched battle of wits and words. Danquah and his supporters had no Press organ of their own but were aided by some newspapers in Accra, and for weeks the battle raged between these papers and the *Accra Evening News*. Nkrumah accused and the doctor counter-accused. Looking retrospectively on that period, one is forced to state that it was a most unfair fight: Dr. Danquah was bound to be defeated. The influence of the *Accra Evening News* was vast and direct, and Nkrumah's continuous tours of the country and his speeches had completely undermined the people's confidence in Danquah.

Nkrumah had other advantages over his opponents. First, though an organised attempt on his part, through the C.Y.O., to coerce the Coussey Committee to publish their report (which he said must recommend nothing short of full self-government) on April 1st, 1949, had failed hopelessly, he still had the confidence of the masses. They asserted that the attempt and the failure were all according to plan. Second, he had just helped a certain U.G.C.C. leader to power through the instrument of his powerful Press. A vacant seat in the Legislative Council was to be filled by a member of the Accra municipality, and the choice had been an African barrister, Mr. Obetsebe-Lamptey, who was among those detained in 1948. With the support of the *Accra Evening News* his electioneering campaign was easy. Very quickly Mr. Obetsebe-Lamptey became known as 'Liberty' Lamptey. Third, Nkrumah could count on his fresh and spotless record and on his ceaseless activity. Finally, Nkrumah possessed a great asset, a peculiar combination of different qualities—youth, vigour, fearlessness, scholarship and brilliance; he had, too, personality, charm and good looks.

By the end of May 1949 the battle of wits had ended, and it was evident that the victor was Nkrumah. Then followed a series of futile efforts to bring about reconciliation; but events had gone too far. Most of the papers pleaded for tolerance and patience, but the *Accra Evening News* was against further delay.

Yet for some weeks after it was difficult to know whether Nkrumah was still a member of the U.G.C.C., whether the C.Y.O. was still in existence or whether fresh compromise had been reached. Certain chiefs advised Nkrumah and Danquah to effect some form of reconciliation, lest the British might exploit the situation to the country's disadvantage.

Gradually, however, it was becoming increasingly evident that the two men could never unite, that sooner or later Kwame Nkrumah would form a rival organisation. Once again reports of compromise were heard, and it was rumoured that Nkrumah was to be the U.G.C.C. general secretary and that the C.Y.O. would not be dissolved. These statements were false.

Attendance at meetings called by the supporters of Dr. Danquah to explain the situation fluctuated—sometimes poor, sometimes encouraging; but even then people only went to boo, challenge or coerce! Those called by Nkrumah were much more successful.

The position of the two camps was becoming increasingly defined. Nkrumah was a lifetime politician; his opponents were in the main professional barristers. The Coussey Committee was still sitting, and the anti-Nkrumah group had to divide its time between serving on the committee and criticising Nkrumah. Each job called for more time than was at their disposal.

IV

THE TEST OF THE TIMES

THE U.G.C.C. spared no pains in telling its supporters that its aim was to achieve self-government for the country 'in the shortest possible time', its leaders at the same time expressing their wish to remain in the British Commonwealth. Most of the members of the U.G.C.C., however, in their uncontrolled enthusiasm, had not pondered over the implications of the proviso, 'in the shortest possible time'. It had been taken for granted to mean *now*. Gradually the people were questioning the exact meaning of that limitation. They wanted to be clear about when it would be 'possible' to demand self-government. They also wanted to know who was to declare that the time had arrived. Such were a few of the questions exercising the minds of most of the U.G.C.C. supporters in 1949.

To many the activities of their leaders were suspect, especially when it was stated that 'the shortest possible time' would be the next five years or more. These suspicions and the challenge to leadership gravely weakened the solidarity of the U.G.C.C. A great deal of distrust was persistently surrounding the activities of the U.G.C.C. leaders, whose past services to the country now became the basis of criticisms and attack by the extreme nationalist papers.

Some of the leaders were accused of being too conservative, too vacillating and pro-British. They could have chosen to ignore it, but it was only too apparent that these insinuations were gaining ground and would have to be stopped. Otherwise they would only have themselves to blame for the consequences. Hence the leaders started to defend themselves on the platforms, through the Press and in conversation. It is a sad comment that while most of the leaders ably defended their integrity and record, a few of them managed to alienate public sympathy from themselves and their organisation. One of these leaders was alleged openly to have described the people as 'Verandah Boys'. Subsequent events were to show the great damage which that charge was to cause. At this juncture it must be borne in mind that Nkrumah was still a member of the U.G.C.C., though without office. Only later did he quit the organisation completely.

The removal of Nkrumah from the office of general secretary had left the U.G.C.C. dispirited and disorganised; but this was not very serious. It was his resignation in August 1949, already referred to, which hastened the decay of the organisation. Prior to his resignation, an attempt to dislodge Nkrumah from Accra had failed, adding one more advantage to his already favoured position.

At last in August the Coussey Committee finished its sittings and handed its report to the newly arrived Governor, Sir Charles Arden-Clarke. Gossip and rumour had it that the committee recommended self-government. The U.G.C.C. leaders properly refused to make any statement. Meantime, the Government went on with its vast programme to guard against any contingency which might follow the publication of the report; preparations which tended to confirm the masses' fears that the recommendation would not be to their liking, and that once again in their lifetime their own people would give them a stab in the back.

The U.G.C.C. leaders, now free from serving on the Committee, started to tour the country; but now the meetings they called were not well attended and seemed to lack vigour and inspiration. Late 1949 found the U.G.C.C. in a pathetic state. We must diagnose fully the causes of this debilitated condition, lest we view subsequent events in the wrong perspective, and a detailed knowledge of the composition of the U.G.C.C. is a great help in understanding the problems which faced its leaders.

It is rather difficult to find the exact parallels of organisations or parties here with those in Britain because those in Ghana are coloured by native characteristics. The U.G.C.C. was what might be described as a Liberal party, and if it compares with any British political organisation, then it is the Liberal Party. It was composed mainly of the middle-classes, or what I choose to call the middle-rich; those who had quite enough for themselves and could save a little every year, and who, compared with the bulk of the population, were rich—though basically they were not. Such classes included chiefly the wealthy cocoa farmers, clerks, artisans and teachers. The U.G.C.C., in addition to these classes, contained a substantial proportion of what was officially described as the 'irresponsible group', or hooligans.

The leadership of the U.G.C.C. was in the hands of middle-class professional men, though a considerable amount of aristocratic blood could be found among them. It hammered out a not too progressive, non-reactionary policy, based as much on conservative ideals as on revolutionary ideas. Its aims were cloudy and inexact, and were neither fervently nationalistic nor anti-nationalistic. The brain behind it, Dr. J. B. Danquah, was a lawyer, a philosopher and an eminent intellectual. Such organisations do not usually have much faithful support—modern man detests parties which try to satisfy every philosophy and appease all creeds and doctrines, having no confidence in midway policies which they feel cannot help them. This was the attitude in the Gold Coast. Most of the people wanted a daring party and a daring leadership. Nkrumah produced both.

On June 12th, 1949, Nkrumah, at a huge rally held at

the West End Arena of Accra, under the auspices of the C.Y.O., launched the first party in Ghana—the Convention People's Party (C.P.P.)—for the U.G.C.C. never was a party and never called itself so. Those at the rally will never forget it as one of the greatest days in their lives. Nkrumah was a member of the U.G.C.C. until August of that year. In what might be described as his most powerful speech since he arrived in the country, Nkrumah informed his audience that he had found it impossible to remain on friendly terms with the other leaders of the U.G.C.C. and that it was imperative that he form a party of his own. He gave some of the reasons for the split and the reasons for his decision. Those were trying times for him and his supporters. Many felt that he had done the best thing. He stressed the fact that his action was inevitable and he convinced them of the necessity of a party 'to fight relentlessly British Imperialism'; one which would dare challenge the Coussey Report when it was published. He asked and gained the sincere support of his listeners. He scorned and satirised their help and promises, to which they unanimously and heartily replied that they would follow him till death. He appealed to them to feel for the new party and to support it as they would support and care for their own children, telling them not to worry about the financial side, for support and faith were more valuable than money; finally he promised them that it would be a party by the people and for the people.

Nkrumah himself knew that he had come to the crossroads in his career, and his adherents realised also that they were giving decisions which would powerfully affect future generations. Nkrumah was slightly nervous—it was a difficult day, but one on which he may retrospectively look today with interest and contentment. His face showed signs of excessive mental and physical strain. He was making history when he said: "There come in all political struggles rare moments hard to distinguish, but fatal to let slip, when even caution is dangerous; when all must be set on a hazard, and out of the simple man is ordained strength."

Hymns were sung, and Nkrumah, the unacknowledged leader of the country, dedicated his life "to fight relentlessly and with all vigour against the forces of imperialism and exploitation". Collections were taken amounting to a considerable sum, although not enough to meet the pressing demand. The meeting was over. The Convention People's Party (C.P.P.), the vanguard of the liberation movement in West Africa, nay in the whole of Africa, had been born.

If the honour of having awakened fervent national consciousness in the Gold Coast people belongs to the U.G.C.C., to the C.P.P. must be given the credit of having kept alive that national consciousness. There followed another battle of wits and words, fiercer and more significant than before. To both the C.P.P. and the U.G.C.C. it meant a struggle for existence and the survival of the fittest. For both it meant either ignominy or honour; but to Nkrumah the loss of the battle could mean the loss of a career. So this time both sides utilised all possible advantages and strategy at their disposal. This was a fairer fight; this time the Danquah group could count on many advantages over their opponents. On this occasion also the local newspapers, with one or two exceptions, came to the aid of Danquah and his comrades.

Danquah argued that in so far as the Coussey Report was not yet published, Nkrumah could not rightly make alterations, and counselled for patience. He denied the allegations of compromise and pro-British tendencies instituted against him and his followers. He explained that they were all against imperialism, and he brought up his past record to show how strong a nationalist he was. He challenged his opponents' uncontrolled encouragement of lawlessness and disorder and of disrespect to the chiefs.

THE TEST OF THE TIMES

In fact, the battle of words and wits nearly ended in a bitter personal affray. Dr. Danquah and his supporters had the backing of the chiefs, the elders and the majority of the more mature in the country, as well as that of the merchants and the small traders, the doctors, the lawyers and other professional men, who one way or the other would be at a disadvantage if there was disorder in the country. This time, therefore, it was not easy to decide who would win.

Nkrumah had the support of what might be described as the masses. They were the underpaid and the underfed; the poor and the needy, the labourers and the petty cocoa farmers, the 'dismissed' and the unemployed; the dejected and the frustrated; in short, all those men and women who, for diverse reasons, strongly resented British rule. He could count also on the solid support of the ex-servicemen and on the backing of a handful of chiefs and professional men. Past records of the Danquah group were questioned and challenged, and the 1948 African Conference invitation controversy was again resurrected, as was the trouble over Sir Sidney Abrahams's invitation and visit. The fact that most of the leaders had served on the Coussey Committee made a subject for criticism, and many other issues were written up in the Press to undermine public confidence in Dr. Danquah and his group.

Whilst the Danquah group asked for 'self-government in the shortest possible time', Nkrumah demanded it immediately; the popular slogan became 'Self-government Now'. Long before the Coussey Report was published, Nkrumah had been impressing upon his audiences that he was demanding immediate self-government and that the committee should recommend that alone, and by every possible means he had sought to make his demands heard by the committee.

He gave reasons for his apparently rash demand. He

said: "We are demanding Self-government now because (*a*) the Labour Government is more favourably disposed because of its Socialist policy towards the immediate solution of the Colonial question; (*b*) if at the General Elections next year the Conservatives were to come into power, our whole struggle for self-government may be suppressed, in conformity with their policy of 'what we have we hold'.[1] In the words of Churchill, 'I did not become the Prime Minister of His Majesty's Government in order to preside over the liquidation of the British Empire'; (*c*) This land of ours is our own and we don't want to continue to live in slavery, and under exploitation and oppression. We want to be encouraged to develop it and live happily in it as free men. It is only under full self-government that we can be in a position to develop this country so that the people of the new Ghana can also enjoy the comforts and amenities of modern civilisation, through the provision of work and fair pay for labour and better conditions of living."

Nkrumah stated openly and quite unreservedly that if the Report did not grant full self-government he would declare 'Positive Action', a 'non-violence sit-down strike, civil-disobedience and non-co-operation campaign'. And everywhere he went he emphasised that either self-government or 'Positive Action' would follow. He gave repeated warnings of his intentions to the Government.

If the previous Administration had been overtaken by events, the new one—the Clarke administration—was determined to forestall them. Before the new Governor arrived in August, his deputy had issued warnings that anyone taking part in strikes for political ends would be dismissed.

Sir Charles Arden-Clarke at once tackled the situation. He stated that any display of force on the publication of

[1] The Labour Party was then in power in Britain and a General Election was imminent within the next few months.

the Report would be met with force and that he would not condone any lawlessness. In order to acquaint himself with conditions in the country he began an extensive tour, during which he formally, and informally, met most of the chiefs.

Other action was taken. A large body of policemen, known as the Mobile Police, was created, trained and armed; barricades were erected in all the main roads and in the streets of the principal towns; the doors and windows of the Government buildings were protected. Recruitment for personnel to man the essential services, should they break down, was started and proceeded swiftly.

Meanwhile, the chiefs once more dissociated themselves in advance from any troubles which might follow publication of the Report.

All the time the battle between Nkrumah and Dr. Danquah was raging. Nkrumah was now becoming more emphatic in his demand for 'Self-government Now' or 'Positive Action'. The doctor abhorred the confusion and disorder into which such a policy might lead the country, and spared no pains to say so.

By leaps and bounds the membership of the C.P.P. was growing; at the same time, Nkrumah was hard put to visit all principal towns to outline his policy and programme and to explain exactly what he meant by 'Positive Action'. Indeed, time was much against him, since soon the Coussey Report was scheduled to be published. Nkrumah's organising powers were put to the test and not found wanting. He had one great advantage: most of the work of organising the masses had already been done—by Nkrumah himself through his C.Y.O. All that was left for him to do was to consolidate that work.

To assess accurately the magnitude of the task Nkrumah performed during this period is not easy. Let it not be forgotten that whilst he was so busy, his political opponents were tireless in their efforts to get the people back into the fold of the United Gold Coast Convention. Nevertheless, with the help of Mr. K. A. Gbedemah, Mr. Kojo Botsio and Dr. B. A. Renner, who lectured in different parts of the country and enrolled members, by the end of October 1949 Nkrumah had welded the C.P.P. into a strong political organisation with himself as Chairman and Botsio as General Secretary.

By this time, too, the party had grown very popular, ready 'to fight relentlessly by all constitutional means for the achievement of full self-government now for the chiefs and people of Gold Coast'.

Other aims were:

> To serve as the vigorous conscious political vanguard for removing all forms of oppression and for the establishment of a democratic government.
>
> To secure and maintain the complete unity of the chiefs and people of the Colony, Ashanti, Northern Territories and Trans-Volta.
>
> To work in the interest of the Trade Union Movement in the country for better conditions of employment.
>
> To work for a proper reconstruction of a better Gold Coast in which the people shall have the right to live and govern themselves as free people.

Finally, the party touched on the delicate problem of the unification of the whole of West Africa into a solid block, which would strive for a place in the comity of nations. For its last aim was 'to assist and facilitate in any way possible the realisation of a united and self-governing West Africa'.

All the time that the C.P.P. was growing, the U.G.C.C. was becoming more and more discredited in the eyes of the people. In fact, in every member which the U.G.C.C. lost the C.P.P. gained a new adherent. The controversy over the C.Y.O. being dissolved had ceased, and there now existed two rival organisations—the old U.G.C.C. and the youthful C.P.P.

Further disappointment for the U.G.C.C. leaders was in store. Just before the publication of the Report, members of the U.G.C.C., as if acting under some charm, began a wholesale exodus from their organisation. First, the branches in the towns started to dissolve themselves; next, this virus of dissolution attacked the villages, and within a few weeks almost all the U.G.C.C. branches were dissolved. Dissolution is perhaps the wrong term—at once these branches turned to the C.P.P.

Meanwhile, the Government was confidently mobilising its forces; likewise Nkrumah, who by this time had so clearly defined his line of action and so well prepared the people that the release of 'Positive Action' had become inevitable supposing the Report did not recommend self-government.

In November the Coussey Committee's Report was issued. It did not recommend self-government. The Governor and some of the officials spoke on it, explained it and counselled for patience and tolerance. They pleaded that the constitution the Report recommended be given a fair trial. And in fairness, one is bound to state that while it did not recommend self-government it brought it within very easy grasp. It thrust a great deal of substantial democracy on the people for the first time in their history; and, it must be said, it was a good and fair Report. It can be summarised as follows:

It made sound recommendations on local government and the setting up of district and local councils.

It made quite commendable recommendations on the central Government.

It agreed on a two-chamber legislature; with the Upper House for the Chiefs and Elders and the Lower House for the 'Commons'. The Committee had agreed on this system of government by a majority of one (the voting was 20 to 19), but thought it necessary to leave the final choice between a single- or dual-chamber legislature in the hands of the old Legislative Council, which contained a substantial majority of chiefs as members, and who, with the exception of the Europeans on it, were all serving on the Coussey Committee.

It recommended the creation of African ministers and the introduction of universal adult franchise in the country; but set the voting age at 25.

It recommended the retention of the Governor's Veto and all his old powers, and made the British civil servants ultimately responsible to the Governor and not to the accredited representatives of the people, the Legislative Assembly.

It recommended the inclusion in the Cabinet of three *ex-officio* members holding the portfolios of (*a*) Chief Secretary, Defence and External Affairs, (*b*) Justice and (*c*) Finance; and made provision for the representatives of the Mines and Chamber of Commerce.

The Report was laid before the Legislative Council for consideration.

A few weeks after its publication, the trouble started. Nkrumah had finished studying it. He argued that once again the chiefs had stabbed the people in the back by not recommending self-government. He accepted the recommendations on the local councils and district councils, but challenged the inclusion of the three *ex-officio* members in the Cabinet and the vast powers vested in the Governor. Finally, he demanded a two-chamber legislature, as had been agreed by the Committee.

All the newspapers, while criticising the report, accepted it wholeheartedly, and pleaded that its recommendations be given a fair trial. Nkrumah's papers—and by this time he had established a chain—bitterly criticised the Report and emphasised the fact that it had failed to recommend self-government. Nkrumah had planned his method of approach to the Report already. He started a tour of the country, explaining to the people that at last their own leaders had let them down badly and that the Report must be rejected.

This strong criticism of the Report soon reached its climax. On November 20th, 1949, the Ghana Representative Assembly, which represented various associations and organisations promoted by Nkrumah, met at the West End Arena, Accra, 'to consider and consolidate all shades of opinion in the country on the Coussey Report on Constitutional Reform in order to enable the people of the Gold Coast to present to the British Government a united front in the demand for self-government now'. The meeting was very successful, though some chiefs and the U.G.C.C. had boycotted it. The recommendations in the report were declared as falling short of the people's aspirations. Nkrumah summed up the deliberations of the assembly, and a resolution was passed that the people of the Gold Coast wanted nothing less than full self-government or Dominion status within the British Commonwealth of Nations. The Coussey Report was rejected. 'Positive Action' was to follow.

The chief advantage that the C.P.P. possessed over its opponents was that no C.P.P. leader was on the Coussey Committee. This was inevitable, for when the Committee started sitting, the C.P.P. had not been formed, and no one on the Committee later joined the C.P.P. after its inauguration. Consequently, although the U.G.C.C. could criticise the Report, and in fact did so, the C.P.P. could cheerfully adopt an altogether stiffer attitude towards the recommendations of the Committee.

British rule in Ghana has not been as despotic and high-handed as some people allege. For any new policy proposed, the British have been careful to obtain the full support of the natural rulers of the people; and that makes it the more difficult to criticise the British for things which went wrong. Their influence and rule have been rather indirect and quiet. The Coussey Report was published with the British Government's comments and suggestions, in which the Colonial Secretary strongly advised a single-chamber legislature and commended the Report for the powers it vested in the Governor.

Whilst the debate on the Report in the Legislative Council was growing tense, the councils of chiefs in the Colony and in Ashanti issued statements that they fully accepted the recommendations of the Committee, and preferred a single-chamber legislature, with all the chiefs and elected members mingled together.

Nkrumah was pressing the country to demand a two-chamber legislature. He may well have foreseen the trouble which would ensue if the chiefs and the 'Commons' were in the same chamber. The *Accra Evening News* explained to its readers that they must not accept a single-chamber legislature, for it would not befit the natural dignity of the chiefs to debate with their subjects. To this the chiefs would not agree, and so the battle continued with the nationalist papers all demanding a two-chamber legislature.

Nkrumah continued to stump the country lecturing the people that since the chiefs had failed them once more they must get ready for 'Positive Action'—a non-violence sit-down-at-home strike, civil disobedience and non-cooperation campaign.

At last the Legislative Council finished its debate on the Report. It made a few alterations. The age limit for voting was reduced from 25 to 21, at the instigation of a youthful member of the council who was the first C.P.P. member to be officially recognised by the Government. More seats were allotted to the Mines and the Chamber of Commerce.

The Legislative Council, which represented the country, had accepted the Report, whilst the people in the main rejected it. The issue was now crystal clear: there could be no self-government in 1949, neither would there be a two-chamber legislature. The report offered Kwame Nkrumah a challenge and he accepted it. The Government waited calmly and the chiefs continued to criticise the attitude to law and order which Nkrumah was advocating.

The most critical month in the year was December. Throughout the country Nkrumah had so worked on the people's feelings and aspirations, that 'Positive Action' had almost come to pass. The Danquah group bitterly attacked Nkrumah's policy, and the learned doctor himself wrote remarkable articles in the newspapers advising Nkrumah to stay his hand or he would throw the whole country into chaos and, perhaps, set the clock of constitutional advance back.[1]

Dr. Danquah philosophised on the alien nature of Nkrumah's policy, arguing that it might suit India or Burma, but would certainly not be of any benefit to Ghana. Some of the newspapers carried headlines announcing splits in the C.P.P., and warned all and sundry not to support Nkrumah. The chiefs issued more warnings to their subjects not to embark on 'Positive Action'. The *Accra Evening News* and other Nkrumah papers were hard put to it explaining their policy and replying to their opponents.

Nkrumah began to issue direct threats to the Government. All hopes of full self-government in 1949 were lost, so he tactfully eased his demands. Towards the close of the year he informed the Government that he would only accept self-government with the portfolio of defence in the hands of the British, but he made one or two other concessions.

The British Government would not agree. They continued to warn all civil servants that anyone taking part

[1] *Gold Coast Express*, November 22nd, 1949.

in strikes for political ends would be liable to dismissal. There followed a series of conferences between the Government, represented by Mr. R. H. Saloway, and the Convention People's Party, represented by Nkrumah. Throughout the conferences, both parties were clearly temporising—the government in order to gain more time to marshal its forces, and Nkrumah in order to organise more effectively his followers and harness them to the impending crusade. The conference broke down; indeed, nothing could be expected of it.

On Christmas Day, 1949, appeared Nkrumah's second Christmas Message to the people of Ghana 'and all men of goodwill'. It was straightforward and gave tremendous inspiration to many. It cautioned them of the dangers and temptations ahead, counselled firmness and courage, and finally reminded his followers not to forget their slogan, 'Organisation', and their motto, 'We prefer self-government with danger to servitude in tranquillity'.

Nkrumah made a final tour of the country late in the month. The situation had become very tense, and it was becoming increasingly clear that there would be a clash. A few days earlier, Nkrumah had alienated all the chiefs by saying in the course of a lecture that 'the chiefs would run away and leave their sandals'; that is, they would embark on voluntary abdications, if not on naked flight. He was believed to have said that they presented no problem to him.

On the first day of the new year 1950, news was flashed through the whole country by one of Nkrumah's newspapers that the alarm had been sounded. Was it genuine? Nkrumah at once clarified the position: it was a false order. A day or two later another alarm was reported, but once more Nkrumah said that he knew nothing about it. By this time European firms in the towns were finding it expedient to close their shops and stores, and although

THE TEST OF THE TIMES

'Positive Action' had not yet been officially declared, the preliminary stage was nearing an end.

At this stage, on January 8th, 1950, just after the locomotive drivers and the railway officials went on strike, Nkrumah, at a crowded meeting of the Convention People's Party held at the West End Arena, Accra, declared 'Positive Action' against the Government. Before declaring it he warned them not to break the law, cautioned them of the 'imperialist stooges' who were trying to undo his work and finally asked for their full confidence.

For the next few days Nkrumah stayed principally at Accra or at Sekondi encouraging his followers. Most people joined the strike at once, but naturally there were some who went to work. All the shops were closed, trade and communications were at a standstill, and it was evident that Nkrumah's policy was succeeding. Government-recruited personnel started manning the bus services, the railways and most of the essential services. The tempo of events was quickening. Nkrumah's movements now became obscure, as he visited the chief towns to see how far he had succeeded or failed.

The Government still issued warnings to civil servants. The chiefs unreservedly condemned 'Positive Action', and gave their full support to the Government in their efforts to break it down. The success or otherwise of the plan was in the balance, for more and more employees began to return to work.

The British then proceeded to act. A state of emergency was declared in the country; the Army took over the capital, and the police units in all the towns were increased. All meetings were banned and Nkrumah's newspapers were suspended. Already arrests of some members of the Convention People's Party in Accra had begun, but no one of the party executive had been touched. Feeling on both sides was running high. For the second time within two years the strength of British arms was being felt. In Kumasi the Mobile Police charged a large crowd which, ignorant of a midnight declaration of the state of emergency, had gathered in a spacious yard, and casualties were considerable. In another town a progressive chief was severely beaten and his palace broken into by the Mobile Police, under the command of a British officer; a British newspaper had to admit the callousness and brutality with which the police had treated the chief and his people. In Accra the police attacked and closed the offices of the *Evening News* and challenged a procession of some ex-servicemen. Some of the ex-servicemen, perhaps from previous experience, were carrying knives, and in the strife which ensued two policemen were killed and a few wounded.

The struggle between the people and the Government continued, but after these incidents the situation gradually eased and life began to return to normal. In an emergency meeting of the Legislative Council almost all the members registered the utter disgust they felt for 'Positive Action'. The councillors promised the Administration their full support, and it was with joy that they hailed the Governor's announcement that the situation was fully under control and that soon the irresponsible elements would be properly dealt with.

By the end of January tension had abated considerably. Nkrumah, Kojo Botsio, Dr. B. A. Renner and several leaders of the Convention People's Party were arrested and charged with sedition and inciting an illegal strike. No disturbance accompanied their arrest, and for some months it appeared as if the party had faded out.

A series of trials of the leaders followed during which an English barrister, Mr. Rewcastle, Q.C., championed the cause of Nkrumah and his men. His efforts were of no avail, and all the men were sentenced to imprisonment. Their terms ranged from six months to three years,

THE TEST OF THE TIMES

Nkrumah receiving the heaviest sentence. An appeal from the magistrate's court to the High Court failed.

One wonders whether the presiding judges and the accused, with their lawyers, and the large crowd of excited spectators at the court, were aware of the great contribution they were making to the history of the new Gold Coast. Certainly Nkrumah and the other leaders of the party became legendary figures, and Nkrumah was the symbol not only of freedom or national rebirth but also of sacrifice and courage. If outside jail he was a problem to the Government, inside he was the very consummation of a puzzle.

Simultaneously with Nkrumah's rise to unprecedented fame and honour came the fall of the leaders of the United Gold Coast Convention. Any meeting which they called was either not attended, or when it was the audience just heckled the speakers. Their planned tour of the country was a complete failure and their inability to enlist mass support at a time when the opposition party was at its weakest showed the utter contempt in which the masses held them. Wherever the leaders went, to explain the circumstances leading to and consequent upon the declaration of 'Positive Action', they were met by hostile crowds.

During these dangerous days a significant event took place which seemed to spur people on to support Nkrumah more wholeheartedly. This was the release of Mr. K. A. Gbedemah, one of the C.P.P. leaders. Had he not just come out of the prison at a moment when Nkrumah and the others were entering it, it would have been difficult for the Convention People's Party to continue its work.

Mr. Gbedemah, as editor of Nkrumah's paper, the *Accra Evening News*, had been sentenced to eight months' hard labour in mid-1949 for libel and sedition, and had finished his sentence in February 1950—the moment that his colleagues went 'inside'. He was at once elected Acting Chairman of the party, and worked untiringly, travelling to different parts of the country, lecturing and organising. We do not know his exact position in the party prior to his phenomenal rise; nor do we know the extent of his influence. But we must accept the fact that Mr. Kobina Agbeli Gbedemah quickly endeared himself to the masses and very soon became known as the 'Second Nkrumah'.

Gbedemah's peculiar advantage was this: he could appeal to the people to have full confidence in the party and its interim leadership, for the sake of Nkrumah, who was languishing in jail. At his meetings Gbedemah fervently expressed himself as the mere deputy of his chief, and his personal modesty deeply impressed his audiences, who began to consider him as the sincere assistant of their leader. None of the C.P.P. leaders had had such a chance to prove their sincerity or capabilities; no one of them had been fortunate enough to act in Nkrumah's stead, and no one of them had ever got the chance to exhibit his organising skill. It was Gbedemah who got this first chance at national responsibility, and he had worked so hard that when Kwame Nkrumah was released the master had nothing but praise for his deputy.

At this juncture, described by C.P.P. followers as the 'darkest days', Mr. Kwesi Lamptey, a middle-aged man who had been residing in England for some years, arrived in the country. The Convention People's Party badly needed strong leadership, and Gbedemah needed an assistant. Lamptey was accordingly elected Acting Deputy Chairman of the party.

Lamptey at once started a newspaper the *Gold Coast Leader*, which gained immediate popularity, for it was very stringent in its criticisms. Nkrumah's *Evening News* was under suspension and the *Leader* came to fill its place. Lamptey toured parts of the country and lectured the people on the need for intensifying the struggle against imperialism, and his fiery manner of speaking was a great asset. It is doubtful whether the Convention People's Party would have stood up against the innumerable odds which were against it during 1950 had it not been for the magnificent job done in those 'darkest days' by these two men; and whilst it is necessary that nationalists should forgo and sacrifice a lot during the struggle for self-rule, it is also just and fair that their past services be noted.

The difficulties which faced the C.P.P. at the time were indeed considerable. The workers who had been dismissed following 'Positive Action' were many, and constituted a problem to the country and the party especially. The leaders of the U.G.C.C. spared no pains to show the futility of the C.P.P. policy, and they cited the position of the dismissed workers to prove how unnecessarily dangerous had been the step which Nkrumah had taken. A 'National Congress' of the chiefs and some political associations mainly of the right-wing denounced Nkrumah's plan and euphemistically called for national unity, but did little else.

With this background story of events in the Gold Coast in 1949 and 1950 in mind, it becomes easier to interpret events in the country since. It becomes easier also to understand why the country's first and subsequent General Elections took their particular course.

V

THE OLD ORDER CHANGES

DURING THE period of 'Positive Action' the Government had declared the Convention People's Party to be a party of the minority; it had described its members as hooligans and irresponsible. Nkrumah before he went to jail had been striving to show everyone, both at home and abroad, that his was the party of the majority. Nkrumah and his supporters did everything possible to substantiate their statements by action, and when the leader had been imprisoned his followers tried to comport themselves in such a way as to disprove the official charges of rowdyism and irresponsibility. The answer to the question whether the C.P.P. had the overwhelming support which it boasted was given when the municipal elections took place in Accra, Kumasi and Cape Coast in 1950.

The results of the election at Accra in April proved that the party really had the support of the people. The electioneering campaign of the party was so effective that most of the candidates of the opposite groups were forced to withdraw. The first victory was won. The Convention People's Party triumphantly swept the polls; indeed, it gained all but one of the contested seats. This was a great day for the party, first because its candidates were now to be in power, and second because the British Government in the Gold Coast officially recognised the party. Nkrumah was never happier than when he heard the news of the resounding victory of his adherents, and this happiness was shared by his friends behind bars.

On June 1st and June 14th the Cape Coast municipal elections took place. Critical observers were ready to com-

THE OLD ORDER CHANGES

ment on any changes in public opinion which had occurred between April and June. Again the Convention People's Party swept the polls, gaining all contested seats. The success of the party at Cape Coast could be attributed to the following causes:

First, the example of the Accra electorate was fresh in public memory.

Second, failure would have meant a positive proof of the allegations of the Government that Nkrumah had no substantial followers in the country—in other words, that the leaders of the country were to be found, not amongst the C.P.P. but amongst the chiefs and their sympathisers.

Third, the candidates of the successful party were mostly young energetic men, who were ready to sacrifice everything for their country's emancipation.

Finally, failure to have registered complete confidence in the 'men behind bars' would have been an underhand blow.

Five months later, on November 1st, the municipal elections took place at Kumasi. The electorate demonstrated their implicit faith in the Convention People's Party by voting solidly for it, following the example of their countrymen in Accra and Cape Coast. They had shown their ardent patriotism; they had not let down their leaders in prison and they presented a challenge to official assertions that the party was unpopular.

No wonder foreign journalists who had travelled to the country to cover the elections had nothing but praise for the organising skill of the C.P.P.

As a result of these successes, it is not surprising that when the first General Election in the Gold Coast was announced to take place in February 1951, the Convention People's Party welcomed the prospect with open arms. The party had been clamouring for the election for a long time, since its executive committee was strongly convinced that they would score overwhelming victory. The municipal victories had struck a deathblow at the opposition and the C.P.P. wanted an early election on as wide a scale as possible; the bigger the election the greater the probability of victory.

As soon as the election dates were made public, the Convention People's Party intensified its propaganda and activities, and began house-to-house canvassing. Most of the people who registered for voting might not have done so had it not been for strong injunctions to them from the party to register and with advice on how to do so. Gradually the mass of the electorate began to associate the C.P.P. with the coming election. Its tri-coloured (red, white and green) propaganda vans and flags could be found everywhere. The flags were displayed on buildings, cars and lorries and were proudly waved by the children. In all their rallies and meetings during these pre-election days, the electorate were exhorted to vote C.P.P. and save their country from foreign rule, for its primary aim was to demand self-government from the British.

The election appeals of the C.P.P. were so direct and so captivating psychologically that they were destined to be fruitful of results. The daily newspapers in support of the party so well prepared people's minds that no room for doubts about the success of the C.P.P. existed; a remarkable job was accomplished by the *Accra Evening News* and the *Ghana Express*. The Convention People's Party had begun a crusade to vanquish all opposition.

The initiative was stolen from the other parties, which, indeed, might very well have been taken as dead or non-existent, had it not been for one or two vans which spasmodically toured the streets of Accra, a few posters in the towns and for the hard work of a handful of faithful and courageous men who, against heavy odds, went about delivering the 'good message'.

The manifesto of the C.P.P. was the first to be issued,

and this bold step became an asset of incalculable value. The manifesto appealed to the electorate to vote for the C.P.P. in order to end misrule by a Colonial Government; it outlined a vigorous and attractive programme of development in all spheres of human activity, economic, social and political, which it hoped to fulfil during its term of office; it promised to achieve Home Rule for the Gold Coast and her people. The manifesto was a first-rate piece of work and though the opposition criticised it severely, their criticisms only served to augment its appeal.

The U.G.C.C. effort, brilliantly written, appealed more to the educated few rather than to the uneducated majority of the country—in contrast to the C.P.P.'s appeal, which was altogether more informal and simple. If the electorate did not listen to the voice of the Convention People's Party and voted for other organisations, the men who had been jailed for sedition would be disappointed, it asserted. As such, the C.P.P. manifesto had a moral obligation attached to it. The masses sensed this and were ready to demonstrate their love for their leaders behind bars.

It was with abundant confidence, therefore, that the C.P.P. finally published, in January 1951, the names of its candidates. It was the first party to do so. The other parties criticised at length the list of C.P.P. candidates, on the grounds that some of the candidates were unfit for the responsibilities they might assume. However, the issue of the names of the candidates of the critical parties did nothing to ease the situation, but instead brought a counter-challenge to their sponsors.

The Convention People's Party looked forward with hope and determination to February. The leaders rightly regarded the moment as the first and, perhaps, the last opportunity to show that the C.P.P. was the majority party in Ghana. Everyone looked forward anxiously to that month as it swiftly drew nearer. Canvassing was at its highest at the end of January, and there were gloomy signs that some unfortunates were destined to lose their election deposits.

The rural elections were held first, and the results, though significant, were not unexpected. The C.P.P. cleared all but three of the contested seats. There were highlights: a prominent chief, much honoured and admired by the Government, fought against a locomotive engine-driver and lost—the chief did not possess the C.P.P. ticket. A young teacher of no special attributes challenged an eminent sociologist holding a doctor's degree and the young teacher won—he was a member of the C.P.P. A little-known young man beat a timber merchant of wide popularity. An unimpeachable barrister had to swallow a direct defeat from a young client. Even the three seats which were not captured by the party were lost only by very narrow margins. These successes were only the prelude to more resounding triumphs.

A day or two later, the municipal elections were held, and once again the results were significant. The Convention People's Party swept the polls, with Nkrumah himself elected by an overwhelming majority for Accra. The elections for the country members were held and the results went only to prove that even the aristocratic and conservative chiefs had to bow gracefully before the political storm.

This is what Mr. Douglas Brown, Special Correspondent of the London *Daily Telegraph*, wrote about the election at Dodowa:

> The scene yesterday at Dodowa, on the green slopes of the Shai Hills, where the paramount chiefs of the Colony met to elect their representatives, was magnificent but full of pathos. The 63 chiefs sat enthroned wearing splendid robes and ceremonial sandals, while behind them were row upon row of their 'linguists' or official spokesmen, each holding aloft his tall staff of office. Opposite this gold

THE OLD ORDER CHANGES

array were grouped incongruously the C.P.P. canvassers, men in grubby white town suits who yet felt themselves to be the ultimate masters. The chiefs were clearly floundering, voting at one moment for some C.P.P. nominee and the next for some notorious reactionary.

When it was all over a note of infinite melancholy was blown upon an elephant horn. The princes rose and, in the shade of their brilliant umbrellas, walked beneath the tall trees as the beating of the drums became fainter and fainter. It was true they were walking towards fabulously large or sleek American cars, and that their wealth and magnificence were still intact. But it was impossible to escape the feeling that these stately, bewildered figures had suddenly lost their political significance.

An absurd situation now existed. The man whose party had won the elections and who had himself been elected by an overwhelming majority was in prison for inciting an illegal strike. However, on February 13th the Governor, Sir Charles Arden-Clarke, as an act of grace in view of the promulgation of the new constitution, released Dr. Nkrumah and his comrades. Great was the jubilation on that afternoon of February 13th, when Nkrumah, a slender figure, came out of James Fort in Accra to meet the wild joy and acclamation of thousands of supporters and sympathisers, many of them weeping, overcome by the occasion.

Led by party vans, the teeming thousands of Gold Coast Africans carried their hero triumphantly to the West End Arena in Accra, the spot where the Convention People's Party had been born, to welcome him home. The ceremony was impromptu, ritualistic and native. A sheep was slaughtered to propitiate the gods and thank them for Nkrumah's return. Speeches, overcharged with emotion, were made by some of the leaders, but the man most involved in the ceremony said little. He thanked his people for their encouragement and confidence, but he was too exhausted and overcome emotionally by the events of the day to say more.

To crown the whole welcoming ceremony, incongruously enough, Cardinal Newman's hymn 'Lead Kindly Light' was sung with pathos and vigour by the wildly enthusiastic crowd. For many of them it was the greatest day of their lives.

The sudden release of Nkrumah from prison had the effect of lowering tension in the country and of improving Anglo-Ghana relations. Moreover, the magnanimous way in which he had been treated by the Governor had to be reciprocated by Nkrumah as a man, whatever might be his general feelings about the British. Mr. Douglas Brown, commenting on this 'act of grace' in the *Daily Telegraph* said, *inter alia*: 'For Europeans this was the friendliest day they have spent on the Gold Coast for years.' He went on: 'African moderates tend to feel that they have been let down.'

The Governor invited Nkrumah to Christiansborg Castle and instructed him to form a Government.

So ended the first General Elections in the Gold Coast. Final results showed that of the eighty-four elected members of the Legislative Assembly (Parliament) over forty-eight were either members of the C.P.P. or fellow-travellers.

The victory of the Convention People's Party had remarkable repercussions on subsequent events. It is the background story of the great attempt towards real democratic government. Many Gold Coast men and women and a few British politicians had been worried in late 1950 at the likelihood of the first Gold Coast ministers being chosen from behind bars; but the composition of the Executive Council (Cabinet) solved this apparent riddle. Of the eleven ministers (excluding the Governor as Chairman of the Council) three were *ex-officio* members, the remaining eight being all Africans, of whom six were members of the Convention People's Party. The two other members were representatives of the Territorial Councils of Ashanti and the Northern Territories. Four of the six C.P.P. members had just served sentences of imprisonment for sedition and other charges. With Nkrumah himself elected virtually Prime Minister, these 'prison graduates'[1] and their associates started the task which was destined to achieve independence and freedom for the people of their country.

[1] This term is applied by the C.P.P. to those people who had gone to jail for purely political reasons. They were all C.P.P. men. The first 'P.G.' was Mr. K. A. Gbedemah.

VI

NEW TASKS TACKLED

ON FEBRUARY 20TH, 1951, amid gorgeous pomp and ceremony, the first sitting of the newly elected Legislative Assembly opened at Accra. Thousands of people from all over the country had gone to the capital for that great occasion, primarily to catch a glimpse of the man who had come out of prison to be their leader. To most of those who watched the historic opening by Sir Charles Arden-Clarke, it seemed that self-government had come; they saw their leaders led into the Assembly by high British officials—something which they could not have imagined four or five years before.

Nkrumah and his C.P.P. during their electioneering campaign promised jobs for the masses, adequate housing and improved amenities and conditions. The promises given, coupled with the ardent nationalism which they had aroused, had carried them into the Assembly without any serious opposition. The people were now anxious to see the results. They felt that they had played their part, and expected their leaders to do the rest. The C.P.P. leaders had been sincere in their campaign tactics, and once in office plunged with vigour and enthusiasm to acquit themselves and to satisfy and reassure the populace.

A big, multi-purpose development plan (the first of its kind in the country) was at once launched and was approved by the Legislative Assembly to come into effect on April 1st, 1951. The plan provided for the expenditure of about £80 million in the period of 1951–6 on such projects as roads, railways, improvement in medical ser-

NEW TASKS TACKLED

vices, provision of more hospitals and water supplies, erection of Government offices, the building of Government housing estates and the expansion of primary, secondary and higher education facilities. The amount was later revised to £108 million owing to increased costs and further projects. The amount was to be spent in the following proportions:

Economic and Productive Services	19%
Communications	32%
Social Services	32%
Common Services	17%

Everyone was agog with enthusiasm. The country was being developed swiftly, and that was what they wanted to see. To a largely illiterate population definite visible signs of progress were more important and reliable than a mass of statistics which, in any case, would not touch the fringes of the life they led. In the first three years about £33 million were spent and over the whole period the approximate estimated expenditure under some of the more important heads was as follows:

[1] Agriculture	£5,500,000
Electricity	£1,750,000
Urban Water Supplies	£3,000,000
Rural Water Supplies	£2,100,000
Roads	£15,600,000
Railways	£17,700,000
Post and Telecommunications	£16,000,000
Education	£12,700,000
Medical	£5,400,000
Housing	£5,800,000
Offices, Staff Quarters, etc.	£6,300,000

[1] G. C. Handbook of Trade and Commerce, May 1955.

ment plan fund was produced from
out recourse to outside borrowing.
ble by the fact that the cocoa in-
about 70 per cent of the country's
a boom period. Other sources of
were export duty and income tax.

The people of Ghana are by nature keenly interested in education, and parents, however poor they may be, strive hard to give their children at least primary school training. Apart from the advantages which education generally confers, it has in the Gold Coast a social standing attached to it, and the uneducated and the illiterate suffer a severe handicap.

There were, before 1951, a considerable number of primary and a few secondary schools in the country, run mainly by missionaries. At the head of the post-primary educational ladder is Achimota School founded in 1924, a famous co-educational institution seven miles from Accra, and maintained by the Government. To complete education are the Kumasi College of Technology and the University College, situated near Achimota.

The outcry for more schools has been long and unceasing. The C.P.P. had promised free primary education at the election, and it immediately set about fulfilling this promise. The primary and middle school system was quickly reorganised and fees were abolished for the former. Considerable grants were made to the College of Technology and the University College to expand facilities and to ensure that both institutions were financially independent and stable. The output of trained teachers was almost doubled within a short period, by the provision of more training colleges, improvement of existing ones and the setting-up of emergency training centres. Secondary school pupils increased threefold, and to meet the demand new technical institutes were provided. The late Dr. Jeffreys, of the London University Institute of

NEW TASKS TACKLED

Education who visited the country in 1954, reported: "In the whole history of education I cannot think of any other country which can match this record of three and a half years." The Government gave a considerable number of scholarships for studies overseas and at Kumasi College of Technology. By the end of 1951 there were 624 Gold Coast students in the United Kingdom—308 of these were holding scholarships from the Government. In addition to these, there were 106 students in the United States of America. In the following year, 1952, a further 198 scholarships were awarded for studies in the United Kingdom and 25 in the U.S.A.

This tremendous achievement in the field of education, which went far to enhance the popularity of the Government, was due chiefly to the foresight and experience of the Minister of Education, Mr. Kojo Botsio, a fervent Socialist, who has subsequently shown himself in all ministries as a most capable man.

Under Botsio's ministration, the first mass-literacy campaign was launched by the Department of Social Welfare and Community Development in June 1952. It was designed to teach the illiterate men and women to read and write their own vernaculars within a matter of a few weeks. It also included classes in hygiene, home management and child welfare for women. Public-spirited literates took upon themselves voluntarily the job of teaching their less fortunate brothers. By the end of September 1952 over 75,000 men and women had passed through the courses and were literate. The campaign inspired those in the rural districts, especially in the remote villages, to undertake minor projects which would improve their standard of living. As a result, latrines, bush-roads, markets and wells were constructed by the villagers with little help from the Central Government.

It was not, however, all plain-sailing. For one thing neither school buildings nor teachers could cope with the sudden influx of pupils. The Government had to fall back on emergency buildings and untrained teachers, with the result that dozens of schools sprang up all over the country in huts and bamboo buildings, manned by young, amateur staff doing their best to instruct hoards of enthusiastic black children. The people had wanted more and more education for their children and the Government had provided it cheaply. A new generation was being created which would be free from the handicap of ignorance and illiteracy.

Again, through Botsio's initiative, a scheme was evolved whereby over a hundred tailors, artisans, carpenters and shoemakers were trained in Britain. It was a measure which brought the Government much credit, although the cost involved was very high, a fact which evoked considerable critical comment from the opposition parties.

In the matter of communications, by the end of its fourth year of office over 800 miles of new major roads had been built in addition to over 700 miles resurfaced. First-class roads had been constructed from Accra to Kumasi and from Kumasi to Tamale in the north. A further achievement was the opening of a new, first-class coastal road from Accra to Sekondi. Fifty miles of railways were built and realigned. The port at Takoradi was expanded and improved and the construction of a new port at Tema (costing nearly £8 million) was begun. This port is intended to relieve pressure of work on Takoradi and also act as the port for the envisaged aluminium industry on the River Volta.

The health of the people was not forgotten. Twenty-four hospitals had been newly completed or extended by the beginning of 1954, and major extensions to Korle Bu Hospital, the Government hospital at Accra, were undertaken, with a view to making the hospital usable for teaching purposes. A huge, ultra-modern, £4 million hospital, the best of its kind in the whole of Africa, was built at

NEW TASKS TACKLED

Kumasi. In addition, minor dispensaries were opened in the remote rural districts by the Government or by local councils aided by the Central Government. Health campaigns were conducted throughout the country, aimed at mosquito extermination, improving the people's feeding habits and making the bulk of the nation conversant with the ordinary rules of hygiene. More wells were dug in the villages, and piped water supplies were extended to some towns.

Ghana is an agricultural country and is likely to remain so for a long time. Over 70 per cent of the country's revenue is derived from the cocoa industry. The whole industry is owned by the peasants, who cultivate the cocoa trees on small farms, using chiefly labour from the north of the country. The cocoa pod was introduced into Ghana in 1879 by a native blacksmith, who returned from Fernando Po with a sackful of the beans. He planted these in Akwapim Mampong, his home town, and after five years the first harvesting of cocoa in Ghana took place. Today it is estimated that there are about five million acres of cocoa-bearing land, producing a crop of about 200,000 tons per annum.

Cocoa has thrived in the country due to the richness of the soil, the thick vegetation, the huge forest trees which serve as a shade and to the humid, tropical climate. Less than half a century after its introduction in the Gold Coast, the country was producing about 30 per cent of the world's cocoa, and was in fact the world's leading cocoa producer. As a result of favourable world prices, the crop's export earnings rose to £42 million in 1948, £60 million in 1951 and £85 million in 1954, dropping to £71 million in 1955.

This export figure of £71 million for cocoa was out of a total export of £77 million; of this £77 million, £32 million went to the farmers, £1 million was spent on transport and freight charges, taxation on cocoa by the Government took £38 million; and the balance of £6 million was retained by the Cocoa Marketing Board. This heavy tax on cocoa paid for the current development programmes, and other projects, such as the building of the Government-sponsored Ambassador Hotel, the State House and other Government offices. Part of this sum was also used in special grants to the University College and the College of Technology, as well as for scholarships.

For over twenty years the cocoa trees had been afflicted by a virus disease, known as Swollen Shoot, which was rapidly devastating the whole industry. Attempts by the former colonial government to enforce compulsory cutting-out of diseased cocoa trees had met with fierce opposition and, as we have seen, was one of the remote causes of the disturbances of 1948. The C.P.P. during their electioneering campaign promised the farmers that compulsory cutting-out of their trees would be stopped once they were voted into power. The farmers accepted the promise with enthusiasm, for to them the cocoa tree was life itself and a diseased tree was certainly far more useful than an uprooted one.

The farmers were also expecting the C.P.P. to help them out of their difficulty. Nkrumah and his ministers knew that the disease meant devastation to the industry. They knew also that there was no cure for it, except complete cutting-out of the diseased trees. That was the opinion of expert agriculturists from abroad and of those working at the research station at Tafo. By 1953 the eastern region of the country, which was worst hit, was producing about half the amount of cocoa it had produced in 1936, in contrast to other regions which showed an increase in output, due to a general absence of the disease. This trend is well illustrated by the following figures:

NEW TASKS TACKLED

COCOA PRODUCTION: REGIONAL PERCENTAGES [1]

	1936–7	1952–3	1953–4	1954–5
Ashanti	30	48	49	51
Eastern Region	43	20	24	24
Western Region	—	—	17	15
Trans-Volta	27	32	10	10

Thus, by the irony of fate, in the middle of the century, the eastern region, the home of the cocoa pod, was in complete economic devastation. What it lost, Ashanti gained, as the disease had not as yet spread to that area.

The new Government, in conformity with its promises, instituted instead a voluntary rather than a compulsory cutting-out programme with increased compensation payments to the farmers. This was made more palatable by the Government's Information Services which explained to the farmers the urgent necessity for allowing the agricultural officers to enter their farms, examine the trees and cut down the diseased ones among them. By May 1952 the fierce opposition of the farmers had lessened, and the Government found it politically possible to resort to compulsory measures.

By the middle of 1954 forty million trees had been cut down and today about one million trees are treated monthly. This treatment is then followed by a serious rehabilitation programme. For this work, grants of millions of pounds have been made available to the farmers.

The Government also gave over a £1 million grant to the West African Research Institute to expand its activities and to undertake more intensive research. The Institute has produced new types of heavy-bearing, disease-resistant strains, and millions of seeds have been distributed to the farmers. Much work has also been done to encourage the cultivation of other cash crops, such as

[1] *Ghana, A Brief Political and Economic Survey.*

palm oil, coffee, coconut oil, and also of staple foodstuffs such as cassava, plantains, yams and maize.

In the field of housing, the C.P.P. Government met considerable difficulty. The situation in the whole country was deplorable, and was not helped by congestion in the chief towns, especially in Accra, where an earthquake in 1939 had deprived a large number of inhabitants of their homes. In an effort to solve this acute problem, the Government spent thousands of pounds on three experimental projects, all without any definite results.

Advice was sought from world experts, from a United Nations Technical Assistance Committee and from British building societies. Much advice was given, but few concrete results were obtained. From 1951 to 1955 the Government progressively increased its expenditure on the housing programme. The figures below illustrate this:

1950–1	.	.	.	.	£289,000
1951–2	.	.	.	.	£535,984
1952–3	.	.	.	.	£1,037,792
1953–4	.	.	.	.	£1,500,000

By March 1955 about 7500 room units had been provided in the urban districts, whilst the victims of the Accra earthquake had been rehoused in 1250 moderately rented, decent and permanent homes. The C.P.P. Government realises the seriousness of the housing problem and recently, in response to public opinion, reorganised its whole programme towards providing moderately priced housing estates quickly and in considerable numbers for the people.

With regard to industry and general economic development, the enthusiasm and vigour of the C.P.P. Government was tremendous. Once in power, Nkrumah and his ministers set out to fulfil the attractive promises they had given the electorate. There were to be more jobs, no unemployment, great industries were to spring up and

NEW TASKS TACKLED

Ghana was to be transformed into a paradise, particularly after the harnessing of the Volta River.

The Government ordered a most thorough registration all over the country of the unemployed men and women, with a view to providing them with jobs as soon as they were available. Ordinances were passed in the Assembly setting up a number of corporations which were to undertake the rapid expansion of industry.

Ordinance No. 22 of 1951 provided for the establishment of an Industrial Development Corporation (I.D.C.), to secure the development of industry through the investigation, formulation and carrying out of industrial projects. For this purpose the corporation is empowered:

(a) To carry on all activities in connection with the development of industry, including the making of industrial products.

(b) To promote such activities by other bodies or persons and to promote the establishment or expansion of other bodies to carry on such activities either independently or under the control or partial control of the corporation, to give assistance, including financial assistance by the taking up of share or loan capital to such bodies or persons.

(c) To carry on any such activities in association with other bodies or persons (including Government authorities or local government authorities) or as managing agents or otherwise on their behalf.

The government guaranteed the corporation a sum of £4 million to cover initial expenses and provide working capital.

Other boards and corporations were also established, chief of which are the Agricultural Produce Marketing Board, established in 1952, and the National Food Board. The Industrial Development Corporation and the other Boards have in a short time done much to encourage expansion of industry and agriculture.

Either independently or with outside assistance on its own, the I.D.C. now runs a biscuit factory, a modest sawmill industry, makes furniture, runs a large-scale laundry service as well as other minor services. It has also given loans to persons embarking on economically feasible projects which are not large enough to be undertaken by the corporation.

The Agricultural Development Corporation gives advice and financial assistance on the cultivation of other cash crops, such as coffee, coconuts, bananas, pineapples and vegetables, whilst the National Food Board recommends ways and means of bigger production of local foodstuffs and their transportation from the rural districts to the chief centres of population.

In an effort to attract overseas capital into the country, the C.P.P. Government has offered the very generous tax-free period of up to five years for 'pioneer industries', and coupled with this there have been repeated assurances by the Government that foreign industries are welcomed, that they will not be nationalised and that in the event of nationalisation of any industries fair and reasonable compensation will be paid.

In fact, although the Government claims to be Socialist, it does not in the foreseeable future contemplate any nationalisation programme. In a major policy statement to the Legislative Assembly on March 1st, 1954, on the subject of the Government's attitude to foreign investment, Dr. Nkrumah said that the Government was anxious to expand the economy of the country, and had for some time been considering the possibilities of progressive industrial development. He went on: "We are satisfied that there is ample scope for the establishment of many new enterprises. A start has already been made, and the Government proposes to take steps to build up and extend the industrial structure of the economy. In formulating its policy the Government has accepted the fact that it will be many years before the Gold Coast will be in a position to find from its own resources people who can combine capital with the experience required in the development and management of new industries. It is therefore apparent that the Gold Coast must rely to a large extent on foreign enterprise, and the Government is anxious to give it every encouragement." Dr. Nkrumah also emphasised the importance attached by his government to the training of Africans for senior appointments and their employment and advancement by new capitalists. He reminded foreign capital that direct investment in public utility services had not been allowed in the past and that there was to be no departure from this principle. He stated that every assistance would be given to new foreign enterprises in the finding of suitable sites, factories and accommodation, and mentioned the development of new industrial estates.

Dr. Nkrumah concluded: "I am confident that with goodwill and understanding, Government and private enterprise can combine to attain our objective of progressive industrial development." [1]

Overseas expert advice was also sought from Britain and the U.S.A. and in 1953 Professor W. A. Lewis, of Manchester University, was invited by the Government to report on the country's industrialisation. His recommendations which were accepted by the Government, emphasised the need for a large, diversified, local agriculture as a prerequisite to any industrialisation programme, and also suggested the setting up of small industries.

The record of achievement of the C.P.P. Government during its term of office to date, so far as the general development of the country is concerned, has been remarkable. It is a record of which any government anywhere could be justifiably proud, and despite the serious mis-

[1] Statement on capital investment in the Legislative Assembly on March 1st, 1954.

takes in some parts of its programme, especially in the housing field, it can congratulate itself on its foresight.

With the same energy that it had used in tackling other problems, the Government turned its attention to the Volta River Project. The Volta River flows down to the sea from the north of the country through an area that contains huge bauxite deposits, reputed to be the richest in the world. These reserves are estimated at about 200 million tons. For a number of years past, previous governments and nationalists have toyed with the idea of harnessing the waters of the Volta to provide both an aluminium industry and an enormous reserve of hydro-electric power. The C.P.P. Government in its election manifesto in 1951 had, without committing itself definitely, promised the electorate that it would examine the project.

The hope of full employment which the Volta plan would offer fascinated the C.P.P. leaders as much as the unemployed. Dr. Nkrumah and his ministers began to show more interest in the scheme. Expert opinion from overseas, especially from Britain and America, was obtained, and a group of local representatives toured Canada to acquaint themselves with the organisation and business of interested Canadian aluminium companies. The C.P.P. leaders, who had at first been divided over the question of timing and whether or not it was economically and politically reasonable to start the project with so much foreign capital as was envisaged, gradually came to support the scheme once adequate safeguards had been given. Some of the leaders and many people felt that it was a hopeless gamble which would in the end prove to be economic suicide for the Government. Nkrumah, however, argued that his Government had enough political control of the country to prevent any outside capitalists finally holding them to ransom over the Volta Project. His arguments won the day, and in 1953 agreement was

NEW TASKS TACKLED

reached between the Gold Coast Government, the United Kingdom Government and the British and Canadian aluminium companies.

This colossal, £144 million, multi-purpose scheme involves building a new harbour, a town, a hydro-electric generating dam, the electrification of rural areas and the mining and processing of bauxite into aluminium. The project is to be run on the lines of the famous Tennessee Valley Authority (T.V.A.), and experts originally associated with the T.V.A. were invited into the country to advise on the prospects for the Volta scheme.

The British favour the idea, as it will ensure their regular supply of aluminium from a sterling area. At the moment they buy about 80 per cent of their aluminium from dollar areas. The C.P.P. Government is keen on the project because it will offer considerable employment. The scheme will provide a wide measure of industry, improve the rural districts and raise the standard of living. Finally, if it proves successful, the political future of the C.P.P. will, no doubt, be assured.

A Preparatory Commission, which had been working out the details of the project since 1952, published its report in 1956. It is a remarkable feat of examination, statistical research and detailed scientific, medical and economic analysis of a big, complex, hydra-headed problem. At the head of the Commission was Commander Sir Robert Jackson, an Australian engineer, formerly assistant Secretary-General of the United Nations and an ex-senior official of the British Treasury. The report stated that the project is economically sound and gives adequate warning of the changes in the country's life which implementation of the Volta River scheme will bring about. Due to rising world prices, the commission estimated that the work will cost about £231 million and that it will take about eight years to complete. Recent estimates, however, indicate a cost of as much as £300 million.

Although final decision on the Volta River scheme has not been taken, it is highly probable that a start will be made. The Government is eager to establish at the beginning fair and reasonable terms under which it would operate to the satisfaction of all interested parties. It is essential that foreign capital is assured of security.

There has been some criticism of the financial provisions for the scheme. It is argued that whilst the Government will contribute the funds needed for the development of a port, railways, roads and bridges, all essential to the scheme, it will receive only a small share of the profits from aluminium smelting. Open discussion between politicians and economists on the financial provisions of the scheme is to be welcomed at this stage, before any definite agreement is reached between the Ghana Government and foreign capital.

The crux of the problem is that Nkrumah's government is not in a position to undertake the project single-handed. In raising capital for its contribution towards the scheme, the Government plans to seek assistance from local loans, the London loan market and from foreign markets, chiefly the U.S.A.

Here the matter must rest for the present. The vigour with which the first African colonial government has tackled its problems, and the results it has achieved, cannot but be an inspiration to other colonial peoples and to the whole of the black races the world over. Undoubtedly errors have been made, but taking these into account and bearing in mind the background of the C.P.P. leaders, one is forced to the conclusion that theirs is a record of achievement which reflects well on Dr. Kwame Nkrumah, their leader.

VII
THE FINAL STEP

APRIL 1951 saw the beginning of a plethora of political parties in the Gold Coast. Among these may be mentioned the Ghana Congress Party, the Socialist Party, the National Democratic Party, the Northern People's Party, the Anlo Youth Organisation and the Togoland Congress Party. Most of them fared badly at their inception, and practically all but the Northern People's Party, the Togoland Congress Party and the Anlo Youth Organisation died as rapidly as they had been born.

This extremely short life-history was due to a combination of factors. First must be mentioned the Africans' general dislike for anything which smacked of a threat or challenge to constituted authority. To many of the ordinary Gold Coast people in 1951-3, both illiterates and a few of the more educated alike, the existence of a party in opposition to the C.P.P. was a direct challenge to Nkrumah's government, the 'People's own Government', and as the final word was still in the hands of British rule, such opposition parties were considered to be either working in league with the British authorities or at least playing into their hands; both forms of betrayal. The main issue was independence, and as the C.P.P. claimed to represent liberation, other parties, however sincere their protestations, were considered opponents of independence and therefore suspect. The C.P.P. has never been blind to political advantage, and on this occasion, as on others, it fully exploited the situation. To many Nkrumah was more than a political leader; he was considered the national leader of a crusade to free the country from foreign rule.

A further weakness of the opposition parties was that their policies were not clearly defined and lacked enthusiasm and vigour. They were preoccupied with local problems, appeared overcautious and tended to speak in a manner alien to the ears of many of their listeners. Some of them had programmes which tried to cover too wide a field, such as the possibility of a limited constitutional monarchy, seeing how far Socialism and Communism could be introduced in step with private enterprise, the eradication of all bribery, corruption and rowdyism, and the introduction of a marriage law to permit regular and inexpensive marriage with more than one woman (with due restrictions) in order to stamp out the scourge of fornication, adultery and brothels!

Add to all this the fact that the opposition parties generally lacked strong leadership. The leaders, excellent men generally, through no fault of their own, belonged to the favoured educated families, and in consequence their opponents found no difficulty in labelling them as men divorced from the people's cause, the people's sufferings and the people's destiny. Once the label had been attached, their political future was undermined. And to a people to whom rumours meant much, wild stories of constant jockeying among the opposition leaders for supreme leadership did not inspire confidence.

The opposition parties were ill-assorted, ill-organised and with little funds. They lacked a telling Press, whilst the Government had at its disposal a rigid, well-organised machinery of political propaganda, run by paid agents and officers. The C.P.P. was controlled by officers whose business it was to see that the party succeeded. The opposition parties were run in the main by men who had other work to do, and who devoted what time they could to political propaganda.

THE FINAL STEP

The parochial attitude of some of the opposition parties, although it gained for them some regional support, did them harm at the national level. The Northern People's Party, for example, which was formed just before the General Election in 1954, was preoccupied principally with the economic development of the north and with ensuring that adequate safeguards existed to prevent domination by the more sophisticated south. Similarly, the Togoland Congress Party and the Anlo Youth Organisation were concerned primarily with the problems of British Togoland and its unification with adjoining French Togoland.

These factors, plus the C.P.P.'s fervent expressions of the rightness of the course it pursued, made the survival of a strong opposition a practical impossibility. Despite Nkrumah's frequent references at home and abroad to his desire to see established in the Gold Coast a strong alternative to his Government, no effective body existed, either inside or outside the Legislative Assembly until about 1956.

The need, however, was widely recognised and was all the greater in that there was no second chamber to exert the necessary delaying and cooling effect on exuberant decisions taken in the lower house.

The 1951 constitution, meanwhile, had been working smoothly, and there had gradually been forged between Nkrumah and his ministers on the one side and the expatriate civil servants on the other that mutual confidence and trust which was needed to ensure the proper running of the constitution. With an eye to public opinion, Nkrumah had said, just before taking office in 1951: "There must be no fraternisation between our Party members in the Executive Council and the European officials, except on purely official relations, for what imperialists failed to achieve by strongarm methods they will hope to bring off by cocktail parties."

Once in power, however, he realised that he could hardly do without the services and friendly association of the European civil servants.

In March 1952, as a result of negotiations between the Gold Coast Government and the British Government, Dr. Nkrumah was made Prime Minister. This was the first such appointment ever held by an African in a British colonial territory, and although it did not really increase his powers, the enhanced prestige which it brought him, and the country, was a source of great satisfaction to the Gold Coast people.

However, the opposition groups emphasised that what the country wanted was not a mere title but independence. Dr. Nkrumah was also goaded by extremist elements in his own camp. In June 1952, Mr. Oliver Lyttelton, then Britain's Secretary of State for the Colonies, visited the Gold Coast and was met by organised demands from the chiefs and people for immediate self-government. As a result of talks between him, the Governor and Dr. Nkrumah, the Secretary of State agreed that the Gold Coast Government should consult the country and make proposals for further constitutional changes. This was accepted by both Government and Opposition, but trouble arose over the means of consulting the people. The opposition parties wanted a Constituent Assembly to be convened containing representatives of all sections of the population, whilst the C.P.P. argued that this would entail the loss of much time and money, in addition to removing men, needed to become members of the Constituent Assembly, from important posts.

After some discussion and airing of views in the Press over this point, Nkrumah invited all the political parties, councils and other groups to send written views and memoranda to his office to be collated and presented to the British Government. The country responded warmly to this invitation, and over 130 written statements were

THE FINAL STEP

sent in to the Prime Minister's office; among these were statements from the Asanteman Council, the influential governing body of chiefs and elders in Ashanti, the Northern Territories Council, the Convention People's Party, the Ghana Congress Party, the Ghana Nationalist Party, the Trades Union Congress and the Farmers' Congress.

After giving due consideration to the memoranda, the Government published, on June 19th, 1953, proposals for a new constitution. These may be summarised briefly as follows:

(*a*) All the ministers were to be representative; that is, the three *ex-officio* British ministers, responsible for Defence and External Affairs, Finance and Justice, were to be replaced by Africans.

(*b*) An Economic Adviser and an Auditor-General were to be appointed.

(*c*) Defence and external affairs were to be assigned to the Governor, who was to be helped in the execution of his duties by a Deputy, to be appointed.

(*d*) The Government desired to see Togoland, a British Trust territory, integrated with an independent Gold Coast.

(*e*) The Prime Minister was henceforth to be appointed directly by the Governor from the majority party in the Assembly, whilst ministers and ministerial secretaries were to be appointed by the Governor, upon the advice of the Premier.

(*f*) The Prime Minister's powers were to be increased and the term 'Cabinet' was to replace the former 'Executive Council'.

(*g*) A single-chamber legislature, instead of a two-chamber legislature, was opted for.

(*h*) The Government expressed its intention to recognise an official Opposition.

(*i*) The Legislative Assembly was to consist of 104 freely elected members, each member representing one constituency of about 45,000 persons.

(*j*) The independence of the civil service and the judiciary was to be written into the Constitution.

(*k*) The Governor's Reserve Powers were to be retained. Other reasons apart, this was to prove to the United Kingdom Government 'the determination of the Gold Coast to move forward to complete self-government without conflict and in an atmosphere of cordiality'.[1]

(*l*) Finally, the Government requested the British Government to transfer the affairs of the Gold Coast from the Colonial Office to the Commonwealth Relations Office.

(*m*) The country's desire to be an independent nation within the British Commonwealth was reaffirmed, although no specific date for the achievement of this objective was stated.

The British Government readily welcomed the proposals, but rejected the suggestion that the Commonwealth Relations Office, instead of the Colonial Office, be responsible for Gold Coast affairs.

In April 1954 the new constitution was promulgated. It gave the Gold Coast complete internal self-government. It was the transition period constitution—the country's final step forward towards independence within the British Commonwealth. A General Election was to be held in June 1954.

Meanwhile, criticism of the C.P.P. had been growing, especially among the opposition groups. These criticisms were engendered chiefly by the allegations of bribery and corruption among some of its leaders, the ostentatious display of sudden wealth and privilege by a few of the C.P.P. officers, and also by the negative results being achieved in the field of housing, where the Government was conducting some expensive experiments, designed to provide houses cheaply and in adequate numbers.

Added to this was the chaos and confusion following

[1] *Proposals for Constitutional Reform*, Accra, 1953.

THE FINAL STEP

the introduction of progressive reforms in education. Although many parents were happy that tuition fees for the primary schools had been abolished, this did not prevent them from attacking the Government for not providing enough schools immediately to absorb all the thousands of children who wanted to benefit from the programme. Nor did the measures taken by Government absolve it from criticism that educational standards were falling because the children were being taught by ill-trained or untrained teachers, a situation that was inevitable.

Again, the advent of the new order had been so sudden that privileged groups who knew other days could not easily forget the gloom and frustration which had been wrought in their lives by the 'young men' of the Convention People's Party—men and women of obscure background who were now masters of the country. Many in the opposition groups undoubtedly looked on with a feeling of distaste as they watched the chicken they had reared and fattened lay eggs for strangers. The chicken was the country, and the strangers the leaders of the Convention People's Party.

A word about bribery and corruption in the Gold Coast. Admittedly, it exists, but it is rather difficult to assess fully the extent. Both the leaders of the Government and the opposition parties are aware of it. As Dr. Nkrumah has pointed out: "Bribery and corruption, both moral and factual, have eaten into the whole fabric of our society, and these must be stamped out if we are to achieve any progress." It is realised by all sections of the community that bribery and corruption, from whichever quarter they may come, must be stamped out. Moreover, apart from the harm to prestige which repeated allegations of corruption in the public service do abroad, there is also the added effect of lowering public moral standards—apart from the obvious discredit it brings on the name of the party in power.

The climax to the confused and confusing allegations of corruption in high places came late in 1953, when Mr. J. A. Braimah, the Minister for Communications and Works, suddenly reported to the Governor that he had taken bribes from people who had contracts with his Ministry. The Governor, no doubt astounded, directed him to go and see the police. He did so and brought with him a bundle of the currency which he said had been given him. He resigned his office, and testified before an African Commission of Enquiry, headed by an eminent African judge (now Chief Justice), Sir Arku Korsah.

During the sitting of the Commission, Mr. Braimah made serious allegations of bribery and dishonesty against some of his Cabinet colleagues, including the Prime Minister. In a three-hour session, Dr. Nkrumah vehemently denied the allegations, and the Commission's report showed that most of them were unfounded or could not be proved. That there was some political bias in these allegations cannot be denied, but one must admit that the ostentatious display of wealth (wrongly or rightly acquired) by some of the C.P.P. leaders undoubtedly gave rise to many of the rumours, which certainly did some harm to their prestige among the more intelligent. Only minor instances of corruption on the part of two junior ministers could be substantiated. Legal proceedings immediately followed, ending with the imprisonment of those concerned.

The C.P.P. Government as a whole was cleared of the charges, but it is debatable whether, even if they had not been cleared, the results of the General Election, soon to follow, would have been materially affected, since the hearts and minds of the greater majority of the population were so geared on one objective, the achievement of independence.

Prior to the elections, the Government's Information Service again conducted a campaign designed to explain

THE FINAL STEP

the registration and voting qualifications and procedure to the mass of the illiterate population. For their own sakes, the political parties, especially the Convention People's Party, also made certain that the people registered and knew how to vote.

In order to circumvent the problem of mass illiteracy, the Government provided ballot-boxes for the candidates, each box being labelled with the party symbol of the candidate—a fish, cow, cooking-pot, elephant or red cockerel! The same method had been used in the 1951 elections and had worked satisfactorily.

The elections were held on June 15th, 1954, amid scènes of enthusiasm. The C.P.P. swept the polls, though it did not fare as well in the north as in the south, but immediately after all the results were in, it was clear that it had won 71 out of the 104 contested seats.

The balance of seats was held as follows: Northern People's Party (N.P.P.), 12; Ghana Congress Party, 1; Togoland Congress Party, 2; Moslem Association, 1; Anlo Youth Organisation, 1; Independents, 16. One Independent soon crossed over to the Convention People's Party side, giving it thus a total number of 72 seats. Later there were material changes in party allegiance, final figures being:

C.P.P.	79 seats
N.P.P.	14 seats
Ghana Congress Party	1 seat
Togoland Congress Party	2 seats
Moslem Association Party	1 seat
Anlo Youth Organisation	1 seat
Independents	6 seats

As a result of the elections, the Northern People's Party emerged as the main opposition group, whilst the Convention People's Party inevitably took office. Dr. Nkrumah was invited by the Governor to become Prime Minister and form a Cabinet, which he did.

At this stage Nkrumah argued that, as the N.P.P. was a regional party and was not organised on a national level, and also as it could not lay claim to form an alternative government, he would not recognise the N.P.P. as the official Opposition.

The leader of the Northern People's Party, Mr. S. D. Dombo, did not allow this challenge to go unanswered. He appealed to the Speaker, Sir Emmanuel Quist, who finally ruled that the N.P.P. should be recognised as the official Opposition of the Gold Coast Legislative Assembly.

The most important clash between the Government and opposition groups was soon to occur. Discontent with the C.P.P. Government had been growing in Ashanti, and matters were brought to a head in August 1954, when the new Legislative Assembly passed an ordinance guaranteeing a minimum price of 72*s.* per load of 60 lb. of cocoa for four years. This price was to be a minimum, irrespective of the extent to which world prices rose or fell. The export duty on cocoa was raised to finance the Government's development projects. Farmers were expecting a higher price for their cocoa as a result of current high world prices for the commodity, and were disappointed with the price of 72*s.* per load.

This frustration and disappointment was chiefly expressed in Ashanti, which in 1954–5 was producing 51 per cent of the whole cocoa output of the Gold Coast. The Ashantis felt that they were being exploited at the expense of regions which did not produce cocoa, and were highly dissatisfied because they felt that the south, especially Accra, was being developed rapidly with funds derived from their sweat and toil.

This general discontent was soon channelled into the formation of a political movement. In September 1954 a

THE FINAL STEP

new party was formed in Kumasi, the National Liberation Movement (N.L.M.), under the leadership of Baffour Osei Akoto, one of the Asantehene's chief linguists.

The N.L.M. propaganda had much to feed upon. It accused the Government of corruption, nepotism and dishonesty, and of leading the country by dictatorship. It called on the C.P.P. Government's previous record to show how badly it was managing public affairs and particularly public funds. Within a short time the National Liberation Movement had become a wild, rambling mass-movement, with a messianic inspiration to free the country from alleged corrupt rule, and to preserve the dignity and traditional authority of the chiefs and elders.

The Asantehene, after some hesitation, gave his blessing to the N.L.M., and this was immediately followed by the fervent support of many Ashanti chiefs and sub-chiefs and their subjects. The ancient history of the one-time glorious Ashanti nation was invoked to inspire the people, and Ashantis who did not support the movement were regarded as disloyal. The N.L.M. was quickly joined by persons who had axes of their own to grind with the Government—men and women who had been expelled from the C.P.P. for disregarding party discipline or for their anti-party activities, persons who felt that they had not received the right jobs or any jobs at all, and by some members of the middle-classes and intellectuals, who felt that the new order, at least as developed by the C.P.P., was to the country's detriment.

Added to all this were the sensational local and foreign Press accounts of the dawn of dictatorship in the Government of the Gold Coast. For the first time in its history the Government came to know the strength of an opposition party, especially as the minor opposition parties sank their identity and merged to support the National Liberation Movement.

At last, the C.P.P.'s often repeated desire had been met

—to see a strong Opposition established in the country, for the proper and smooth working of parliamentary democracy. It will be for future historians to assess whether or not the C.P.P. leaders saw a threat to their political future in the birth of the N.L.M. Certainly, the opinion of many people in the south was that the N.L.M. would sooner or later—rather sooner than later—go the way of all earlier post-C.P.P. parties and fizzle out. In this opinion they were to be proved wrong.

Dr. Nkrumah made some attempt to appease the N.L.M. early in 1955 by raising the cocoa price from £134 to £149 a ton, i.e. from 72*s*. to 80*s*. per load of 60 lb. But times had changed and even this increase would not satisfy the new-found opposition. The issue was no longer an economic one but had become political, and the original demands had by this time been lost in a welter of serious political and constitutional issues. Even the institution of a salary of £600 per annum for the chiefs did not produce any ameliorative effect on their critical attitude.

The N.L.M. now demanded a federal government in which Ashanti, as one federal region, would have more control over her own finances. It also demanded a two-chamber legislature, in which the chiefs would have a definite place. The N.L.M. simultaneously asked for commissions of enquiry into public boards and corporations, and for the investigation of alleged misuse of public funds.

Their demands grew more and more vocal and vehement; it was very clear that the militant spirit of Ashanti was awake. Membership of the National Liberation Movement grew by leaps and bounds and the inflamed outlook of the new party was exemplified by instances of thuggery against political opponents, periodic assault and beating of persons who professed C.P.P. views and the dynamiting of houses of that party's known leaders and supporters. This met with considerable retaliation. Within

THE FINAL STEP

a short time the C.P.P. had become an underground movement, not daring to show its head in Ashanti, where it became unsafe for its leaders to visit; indeed, feeling became so hot that there was a mass exodus south of C.P.P. adherents—to a cooler political clime.

The subsequent catastrophic fall in world cocoa prices in 1956 only went to show the wisdom of the C.P.P. measure a couple of years before in putting to reserve so much of the money derived from the cocoa trade when it was having a boom.

As the popularity of the N.L.M. grew, other bodies, which had no direct interest in the cocoa issue, joined forces with the movement. Although the north does not produce cocoa, and although it would certainly be the loser under a federal system of government, this did not prevent the leaders of the Northern People's Party (the N.P.P.) from casting in their lot with the N.L.M. The general backwardness of that region was apparently to be laid at the door of the C.P.P. It appeared that all the parties and groups were out for a kill and that the C.P.P. was to be the victim. It seemed that progressive and reactionary elements were ready to align together for that one purpose.

In October 1954 the Asanteman Council formally petitioned the Queen for a Commission of Enquiry into the possibilities of a federal form of government for the country. The British Secretary of State, replying in January 1955, said that as the Gold Coast was self-governing the matter was one to be settled by the Gold Coast Government, not by Britain.

Nkrumah's reaction to the petition was that for a small country like the Gold Coast, with a population of about five million and having a homogeneous, closely associated people, federation would be impracticable and unwise. At best he was prepared to concede a considerable measure of regional devolution. To that end he invited the N.L.M.

and the Asanteman Council to discuss the matter, but both rejected his invitation.

The Government then appointed, in April 1955, a select committee of the Legislature to consider the question of a federal government and the matter of a second legislative chamber. Opposition members of the Legislative Assembly refused to serve on the committee, in the belief that it had prejudged the issues at stake. The committee, headed by Mr. C. H. Chapman, came out strongly against federation, but advised the establishment of regional bodies to work in association with the Government in the development, planning and execution of industrial projects.

Late in 1955, at the request of the Gold Coast Government, a constitutional expert, Sir Frederick Bourne, visited the country to advise the Government and other interested parties on regional devolution of powers. The Asanteman Council and the N.L.M. refused to take part in these formal joint discussions. The two bodies felt that the passing of a Bill, shortly after Sir Frederick's arrival, to allow minor chiefs in Ashanti to appeal directly to the Governor for the settlement of 'destoolment' and other local constitutional disputes, instead of appealing to the Asanteman Council, as had hitherto been the case, showed bad faith on the Government's part. Despite the initial setback he experienced, Sir Frederick went ahead with his enquiries, and in December 1955 presented a report to the Government of the Gold Coast, which accepted it in principle.

The report recommended very substantial transfer of power from the centre to the regions. It suggested the establishment of regional assemblies, to be made up of the region's own representatives in the Legislative Assembly, from local councils in the region, and from co-opted members.

The assemblies, Sir Frederick suggested, should be

THE FINAL STEP

given grants and should have considerable responsibility so far as development and social services were concerned. They should also have representatives on the various corporations and public boards. Concerning the position and status of chiefs, he suggested that no measure designed to affect the position, traditional functions and privileges of chiefs should be introduced in the Legislative Assembly until the appropriate state councils had been consulted.

The N.L.M. felt that the proposals were inadequate to ensure complete protection of the interests of the regions, and pressed for the calling of a Constituent Assembly. Nkrumah agreed to the calling of an inter-party conference representing diverse groups and opinions.

The Conference was held at the Assembly Hall of Achimota School, and thus later became known as the Achimota Conference. It was headed by an eminent Gold Coast public servant, Mr. C. W. Tachie-Menson. The primary duty of the Conference was to examine the recommendations of Sir Frederick Bourne, who was present at the Conference to offer advice where required. Once again the N.L.M. and the Asanteman Council boycotted the Conference. After a month's sitting, on March 16th, 1955, it concluded its work by accepting the general pattern of Sir Frederick's proposals with some modifications.

In April 1956 the Government published its proposals for the establishment of independence and also its comments on the Achimota Conference recommendations. The Report was accepted with a few recommendations. The Government believed that the advance to independence could be effected by appropriate modifications in the existing constitution and by the adoption of conventions which had grown up in the United Kingdom. Under the new proposals, the Gold Coast was to become an independent member state of the British Commonwealth under the name of Ghana. A Governor-General, appointed by the Queen at the instance of the Gold Coast

Government, was to act in all matters on their advice. Supreme legislative power was to be vested in the nation's Parliament, whose life should be five years. The independence of the public service and the judiciary was to be guaranteed. The country was to be responsible for its own defence. The constitution could not be amended without the consent of a two-thirds majority of the members of Parliament present and voting. Six regions were to be established. The future of the chiefs was to be adequately safeguarded, whilst freedom of conscience and religion was to be explicitly written into the constitution.

The proposals were debated in the Legislative Assembly on May 18th and 22nd, 1956. The opposition boycotted this debate. These proposals were, however, generally acceptable to the country, including the opposition groups; but the latter insisted that the question of the form of the constitution should be settled definitely before independence, and not after, as proposed by the Government.

The N.L.M. and its allies now demanded either a referendum or a General Election to settle the issue, and were prepared, if all else failed, to secede Ashanti completely from the rest of the country. The C.P.P. Government maintained that just a couple of years previously it had been given a clear mandate at a General Election to achieve independence for the people within the life of its Assembly, and therefore another election was unnecessary. Moreover, it argued that the state of the country would make the proper holding of democratic elections impossible; whilst there was also the likelihood of some interested groups exploiting the inflamed state of Ashanti to plunge the whole country into disturbance. It therefore refused to hold the elections. By this time, attacks by the N.L.M. and other opposition parties had become very bitter.

Meanwhile, the Government and the Colonial Office in

THE FINAL STEP

London were in constant communication over the whole issue, and at the height of the controversy Nkrumah sent his right-hand man, Kojo Botsio, to London by air to see the British Colonial Secretary and explain to him personally his Government's stand over the issue.

On May 11th, 1956, the Colonial Secretary, Mr. Lennox-Boyd, announced in the House of Commons that because of the failure to resolve the constitutional dispute, the aim of early independence could only be achieved after the peoples of the Gold Coast had had 'a full and free opportunity to consider their constitution and to express their views on it'. The statement added that the British Government would be ready to accept a motion, passed by a reasonable majority in a newly elected Legislature, calling for independence within the Commonwealth, and would declare a firm date for that purpose. The announcement caused much stir in the country, and the N.L.M. considered they had won a moral victory.

The political parties immediately began to mobilise their forces. The election was to be fought over the issue of a federal or unitary constitution for the country. The C.P.P. campaigned for a central government, whilst the opposition groups advocated federation. Although it was still not clear what constituted 'a reasonable majority', it was becoming increasingly accepted by both groups that a simple, clear majority would have to be taken as 'a reasonable majority'.

The election was held on July 12th and 17th, 1956, and despite many indications that the results might not be decisive, Nkrumah's Government was returned with a large majority. Nkrumah himself was elected once more by an overwhelming majority for a constituency in Accra. Of the 104 contested seats, the C.P.P. won 71, the Northern People's Party 15, the National Liberation Movement 12, the Togoland Congress Party 2, the Moslem Association Party 1, the Federation of Youth

THE NEW GHANA

Organisation 1 and Independents 2. One Independent later joined the C.P.P.

The C.P.P. gained all seats except one in the south. Although it lost a number of seats in Ashanti, even there it held 8 out of the 21 seats and won 43 per cent of the total vote. In the Northern Territories the C.P.P. won 11 out of 26 seats and 8 out of 13 in the Togoland region.

The election results showed that the great majority of the people were solidly behind the Convention People's Party. They also showed that the very fact that the opposition groups were regional was their weakness, in that they did not command general and widespread support.

From this General Election emerged a strong and fierce, well-organised Parliamentary Opposition, led by Dr. Kofi Busia, a sociology professor of the local University College. Included in its ranks were locally well-known intellectuals such as Dr. Kurankyi-Taylor, Mr. Kobina Kessie, Mr. Victor Owusu and Mr. Joseph Appiah, whose marriage a few years earlier in Britain to Miss Peggy Cripps, daughter of Britain's one-time Socialist Chancellor of the Exchequer, the late Sir Stafford Cripps, had caused considerable comment in the world Press.

Although the 1956 election did not materially change the strength of the C.P.P. in the Legislative Assembly and although the popularity of the Government was increased, three of Nkrumah's colleagues were not available for office in his new Cabinet.

These men, whose sense of duty had elicited much favourable comment during their terms of office, were Mr. Asafu-Adjaye and Mr. J. E. Jantuah, who represented Ashanti constituencies, and Mr. Imoru-Egala, who came from the north. Mr. Asafu-Adjaye had not sought re-election, and after a brief period as a director of the

THE FINAL STEP

local national bank was appointed Ghana's first High Commissioner in London, with Mr. Jantuah as his deputy.

To middle-aged Achimota-trained Imoru-Egala went the all-important job of the Chairmanship of the Ghana Cocoa Marketing Board, which is responsible, by statute, for the buying and sale overseas of Ghana cocoa. The Board, which has assets of over £200 million sterling invested mainly overseas but to some extent locally, is now the sole creditor of the Ghana Government. As cocoa is the economic life-blood of the country, it is apparent that he who controls the Ghana Cocoa Marketing Board controls Ghana! Nkrumah's complete trust and confidence in Mr. Egala is obvious; what is more, this signal appointment of a man from a region which does not produce a single bean of cocoa to the Chairmanship of the Board controlling the whole industry has done more than anything else to assure the hesitating northerners that the men at the helm have their welfare truly at heart.

Nkrumah's appointments have sometimes caused violent criticisms from the Opposition, but Mr. Egala's elevation to that vital post has been accepted by all sections as the most statesmanlike, politically acute and wisest appointment he has made. By this act alone, the rumours of bribery and corruption, ineptitude and nepotism, which have surrounded the Board's activities during a certain period of its existence, have disappeared into thin air.

The final step in the country's constitutional march was taken on August 3rd, 1956, when the new Government introduced a motion in the Legislative Assembly asking the British Government to provide for the independence of the Gold Coast as a sovereign state within the Commonwealth under the name of Ghana.[1] The motion was

[1] Long before the Gold Coast became Ghana, local politicians had been calling the country that name for purely sentimental

passed unanimously, as the Opposition did not attend the debate.

The British Government considered that the outcome of the election and the subsequent vote on the motion fulfilled the conditions of the Colonial Secretary's undertaking on behalf of the British Government given on May 11th, 1956. Consequently, the Colonial Secretary, in a dispatch to the Governor dated September 15th, 1956, replied that the majority in favour of the motion must clearly be regarded as reasonable, that the British Government would at the first available opportunity introduce into Parliament a Bill to accord independence to the Gold Coast, and that subject to parliamentary approval the British Government intended that independence should come about on March 6th, 1957.

The great news was released dramatically to the people of the Gold Coast on September 18th, 1956, by the Prime Minister, in a speech to the Legislative Assembly. The whole House was tense. A great day in the life of the country was in sight. The uproarious reception given to the announcement by both sides of the House, and the tremendous ovation given to Nkrumah by an excited crowd outside Parliament House in Accra, were indications that at last the wish of the people was to be achieved. The first African territory under colonial rule to become independent was about to be born.

and political reasons. The name had originally been suggested by Dr. J. B. Danquah and the idea was accepted by Dr. Nkrumah.

The experts are not agreed on the origin of the present Ghana people and their claim to originate from the great Ghana Empire which flourished in the Sahara and Sudan in the second century. However, there seems to be some evidence in support of this, strengthened by local lore.

VIII

DEADLOCK!

THE BIRTH of the new nation of Ghana was not going to be easy. After the election, the Opposition sent a delegation to London to make representations to the Secretary of State for the Colonies that the interests of tae regions be securely guaranteed before independence was proclaimed. In the light of the British Government announcement, however, the Opposition began to drop is demand for federation, but continued to insist on full agreement over the form of the constitution before independence. In a letter to *The Times*, September 22nd, 1956, Dr. K. A. Busia said that their aim was an agreed constitution that safeguarded the minority rights of the Northern Territories, respected the identity of the Ashanti nation, provided for an independent judiciary and secured the legal freedom of all citizens. Dr. Nkrumah made another effort to meet the Opposition demands, and in October 1956 a series of talks on the constitution were held between the representatives of the four territorial councils, the parliamentary Opposition leaders and the Government.

On November 7th, 1956, as a result of these talks, the Government published revised proposals for the constitution of Ghana, together with an appendix summarising the chief points of difference between it and the Opposition. These new proposals were debated by the Legislative Assembly from November 12th to 14th, and were approved by a vote of 70 to 25. The Gold Coast Government then submitted them to Britain, requesting the British Government to enact an Order in Council to come into effect on the date of independence, based on the revised proposals as approved by the Assembly. Meanwhile, the Opposition refused to accept them, and even threatened the secession of Ashanti and the Northern Territories should agreement not be reached before March 6th, 1957, the appointed Independence Day.

In November 1956 a joint resolution was sent to Britain by the National Liberation Movement and the Northern People's Party, asking for a separate independence for Ashanti and the Northern Territories and for a Partition Commission to divide the assets and liabilities of the Gold Coast among its four component territories The secession movement had the support of Baffuor Akoto and the Asanteman Council, but not of Professor Busia, who maintained that adequate safeguards for individual and minority rights and effective powers for the regions should be written into the constitution. The opposition groups would not budge an inch, neither was the Convention People's Party prepared to compromise. A complete deadlock had been reached.

The British Government replied in December 1956 to the secession demands, stating that it did not consider partition in the interests of the country as a whole or of its component parts. The Opposition was still dissatisfied. March 6th, 1957, was fast approaching, yet the constitutional deadlock showed no signs of being solved within the next couple of months. Meanwhile, preparations for the celebration of the great day were going on at great speed.

At this stage it was suggested in some responsible quarters that it would be in the country's best interests in the Colonial Secretary himself came to the Gold Coast to help solve the constitutional deadlock. Both the Government and the Opposition saw the wisdom of such a move and accordingly Nkrumah invited the British Colonia Secretary, Mr. Lennox-Boyd, who was about to pay a visit

DEADLOCK!

to parts of Central Africa, to visit the country and help to smooth out the constitutional differences. The Colonial Secretary accepted the invitation and visited the Gold Coast from January 24th to 30th, 1957. He held talks with the Government and the Opposition leaders, the Asantehene and other chiefs and leaders, and visited the north and other regions to consult with the leaders. Despite many apparent differences of view and some lack of mutual confidence between the different parties, Mr. Lennox-Boyd was very conscious throughout his visit of an underlying unity of purpose. All those whom he met were united in their great desire that Ghana should make a successful start to its independent life.

In presenting the Proposed Constitution, which was the result of his talks, he expressed his confidence that the plan provided reasonable safeguards against abuse, and that it was a fair and workable foundation on which the people of Ghana would be able to build their independent nationhood within the British Commonwealth.

After a brief visit to Britain of two Gold Coast ministers, Mr. Kojo Botsio and Mr. Gbedemah, a White Paper outlining the proposed constitution for Ghana was published on February 8th, 1957. Although the British Government still had the final say in the Order in Council embodying the constitution, the White Paper stated that 'in drafting the constitution the United Kingdom Government had naturally taken the fullest possible account of the views of the Gold Coast Government'.

The constitution was finally embodied in an Order in Council published on February 22nd, 1957. Its provisions showed that Mr. Alan Lennox-Boyd had done a great deal to bring the opposing camps closer together. It was a personal triumph in diplomacy. Both sides were able to give in here and there without losing face, due chiefly to Mr. Lennox-Boyd's presence and advice, though the part played by an ex-Labour M.P. from Britain, Mr. Geoffrey

Bing, Q.C., was considerable. The deadlock had been solved, and the future of the new nation yet to be born was certainly brighter than it had appeared a couple of months before.

The Constitution of the Independent State of Ghana may be summarised below briefly as follows:

> Ghana is an independent state 'within the Commonwealth with the Queen as Sovereign and with a cabinet and parliamentary system of government of the same general type as is found in the United Kingdom and other independent Commonwealth Countries'.

1. *The Executive*

The executive power is vested in the Queen, represented in Ghana by a Governor-General, appointed by Her Majesty in accordance with the conventions obtaining in other Commonwealth countries. The constitution provides that the powers and functions of the Queen and the Governor-General be exercised as far as may be in accordance with the constitutional conventions which apply in Britain, except where there is expressed provision to the contrary. The salary of the Governor-General is statutory expenditure and is not to be diminished during his period of office. A Cabinet of at least eight ministers drawn from the Members of Parliament and collectively responsible to Parliament is provided for, whilst ministers are appointed and removed by the Governor-General on the advice of the Prime Minister. The Governor-General shall terminate the Prime Minister's appointment if at any time the National Assembly passes a vote of no confidence in his Government unless within three days the Prime Minister advises the Governor-General to dissolve the Assembly.

2. *The Legislature*

Supreme legislative power is vested in Parliament con-

DEADLOCK!

sisting of Her Majesty the Queen and the National Assembly.

The Assembly consists of a Speaker and not less than 104 members. Bills passed by the Assembly and assented to by the Governor-General in Her Majesty's name become Acts of Parliament. The maximum life of the National Assembly is five years instead of the previous four years; and there is to be a session of the Assembly at least once a year. Any citizen of Ghana aged 25 years or over who can speak and read English is eligible for election.

The Members are elected by secret ballot on the basis of universal adult suffrage. Freedom of religion is guaranteed and no laws can be made discriminating against any racial community. The constitution provides that no Bill to amend, repeal or modify any part of the constitution shall be presented for the Royal Assent unless it has on its third reading received a two-thirds majority vote in the House.

Additional processes are required when a Bill seeks to amend, repeal or modify certain basic, entrenched clauses of the constitution dealing with subjects such as racial discrimination, change of constitution, freedom of conscience, calling of a General Election, the Public Service and the Judiciary. As regards the Regional Assemblies and the states of chiefs in such matters, on report after the committee stage in the National Assembly the Bill in question must be referred to all the Regional Assemblies and the Houses of Chiefs. In each region the House of Chiefs may within one month submit its views to the Regional Assembly, which after taking account of those views shall within three months of reference to them express by a simple majority its approval or disapproval of the Bill as it stands. When the Assemblies of two-thirds of regions have expressed their approval of the Bill, the third reading can be taken in the National Assembly, where to become law it shall require the support of two-thirds of the members of the Assembly. Any Bill for the abolition or suspension of a Regional Assembly, or for diminishing its functions or powers, requires the consent of the Regional Assembly of the region concerned. If it is rejected by that Assembly it may be submitted to a referendum in the region, and if approved by simple majority vote, this then is regarded as constituting the required approval of the Regional Assembly. Emergency powers, subject to the constitution, are conferred upon the Governor-General, and adequate safeguards against compulsory acquisition of property are guaranteed; so is the right to claim appropriate compensation, and the right to appeal to the courts for redress of grievances over the acquisition or the amount of compensation paid.

3. *The Public Service*

The Ghana Constitution provides for a Public Service Commission, members of which are appointed by the Governor-General on the advice of the Prime Minister. The appointment, promotion, transfer, termination of appointment, dismissal and disciplinary control of public officers is vested in the Governor-General, acting on the advice of the Public Service Commission, except for the posts of Permanent-Secretary and of corresponding or higher grades in the Public Service and special overseas posts. With regard to such posts, the Governor-General acts upon the Prime Minister's advice. Regulations affecting the Public Service are made by the Governor-General acting on the advice of the Public Service Commission. The interests of expatriate civil servants are not neglected, for the constitution provides for the payment of appropriate compensation to those appointed before March 31st, 1954, who decide to retire from the Ghana Public Service.

DEADLOCK!

4. *The Judiciary*

The independence of the judiciary is guaranteed in the constitution. The appointment, promotion, transfer, dismissal and disciplinary control of judiciary officers (other than judges) is vested in the Governor-General acting on the advice of the Judicial Service Commission, which consists of the Chief Justice, the Attorney-General, the senior Puisne Judge, the Chairman of the Public Service Commission and a person who is or shall have been a judge of the Supreme Court appointed by the Governor-General, acting on the advice of the Prime Minister. Regulations governing the judiciary are made by the Governor-General on the advice of the Judicial Service Commission. The Chief Justice and (when they exist) Justices of Appeal are appointed by the Governor-General acting on the advice of the Prime Minister; whilst Puisne Judges are appointed by the Governor-General upon the advice of the Judicial Service Commission.

Any judge is liable to removal from his office, on an address of Parliament carried by not less than two-thirds majority in the House, on the ground of stated misbehaviour or of infirmity of body or mind. Judges are to retire at the age of 62, unless permission is granted to a judge by the Governor-General to continue in office for a further specified period subject to continued mental and physical health. Provision is made for compensation to judges from overseas who retire before the age of 60. The constitution also provides for the setting up of the Ghana Court of Appeal, from which appeals can be made to the Privy Council in the United Kingdom.

The Attorney-General continues as a member of the Public Service, although provision is made for the future assignment of that office to a Cabinet Minister. This will be done only after due consultation with the Opposition.

5. *The Regions* and *Regional Assemblies*

The constitution provides for the division of Ghana into five regions: Eastern, Western, Trans-Volta-Togoland, Ashanti and the Northern Territories, with their present boundaries. These boundaries cannot be altered without the consent of the region or regions concerned, either by a majority vote in the Regional Assembly and subsequently through the National Assembly or by a regional referendum to be followed by a majority vote in the National Assembly. If, however, the proposed alteration in boundaries should result in an increase in the number of regions, a referendum must be held in all existing regions. A simple majority of votes cast in favour of change will necessitate the proposal being put before all Regional Assemblies. Contingent on their approval by simple majorities and provided always that two-thirds of the regions have approved the referendum, then the whole question of an increase in regions, resulting from a change in boundaries, must be put before the National Assembly, where a simple majority can confirm the change in law.

It is obvious that the idea here is to ensure that changes in regional boundaries cannot be made thoughtlessly. By stating explicitly that there should be five regions, the Government gave up its earlier demand for a separate Brong Region, as an offshoot of Ashanti. However, this question is not yet closed and could be reviewed in the light of the appropriate constitutional clauses stated above.

A Regional Assembly is established in each of the five regions, and each Regional Assembly has vested in it by authority functions and authority relating to:

(*a*) Local Government.
(*b*) Agriculture, Animal Health and Forestry.
(*c*) Education.
(*d*) Communications.

DEADLOCK!

(e) Health and Medical Services.
(f) Public Works.
(g) Town and Country Planning.
(h) Housing.
(i) Police.
(j) Such other matters as Parliament may from time to time determine.

The maximum life of the Regional Assemblies is three years, and recommendations on their composition, authority, functions and powers have been made by a Regional Constitutional Commission, headed by Mr. Justice W. B. Van-Lake. Until such time as the permanent establishment of the Regional Assemblies is effected, Interim Assemblies have been formed consisting of M.P.s for each region.

6. *Chieftaincy*

The chiefs have been the traditional rulers of the country from time immemorial and were recognised as such by the British Government. It was through them that the British administered the Gold Coast. This system of indirect rule alienated many of the people from their chiefs. Moved by the oratory of Nkrumah and his friends, many people were beginning by the end of 1950 to associate the chiefs with British rule. The situation was worsened by the rather too close friendship between some of the chiefs and the British officers, by a statement from Nkrumah to the effect that reactionary and other chiefs who refused to move with the people and the times would be 'destooled', and by the spasmodic waves of 'destoolment' of chiefs which swept the country between the period 1949 to 1952. The chiefs, therefore, felt that their position was at stake; that their institution was in danger of being abolished. Consequently, from 1949 to 1956 they sought every opportunity during revision of the country's constitution to seek specific assurances that they would enjoy a proper status in society. This uncertainty about the future sometimes took the form of demands for a separate Upper House, sometimes for the inclusion of the chiefs and the elected 'Commons' in the same House. But in whatever form it expressed itself this general gloom about the future was always apparent.

The new constitution completely allays and dispels these fears. It guarantees the office of Chief in Ghana existing by customary law and usage. It provides for a House of Chiefs to be established by Act of Parliament for each region. There will be a Head of each region, who shall, for Ashanti, be the Asantehene, and for the other regions a person chosen by the Houses of Chiefs. A House of Chiefs will have power to consider any matter referred to it by a minister or the Assembly, and may at any time offer advice to any minister. The constitution contains provision for dealing with appeals from traditional councils in matters of a local constitutional nature which will be defined in the following terms:

(*a*) The nomination, election or installation of any person as a chief or the claim of any person for election to the position; or

(*b*) The deposition or abdication of any chief; or

(*c*) The right of any person to take part in the election, or the installation of any person as chief; or

(*d*) The recovery or delivery of stool property or skin property in connection with any such election, installation, deposition or abdication; or

(*e*) Political or constitutional relations under customary law between chiefs.

Appeals from State Councils will be made to the Houses of Chiefs of the region in which the issue has arisen, who will be obliged within a prescribed period to refer the appeal to an Appeal Commissioner appointed by the Judicial Service Commission. It will be permissible for the Appeal Commissioner to sit with assessors or to call on

DEADLOCK!

any person to give him advice on local law and custom. The Appeal Commissioner will transmit his report and findings to the House of Chiefs, which will not have the power to depart from his findings but may re-submit the matter to him for further clarification. In the case of matters heard in the first instance by the House of Chiefs for the Ashanti Region, or by a committee of that House, an appeal shall be laid before an Appeal Commissioner, who will forward his report and findings to the Head of the region. He in turn will act in the same way as provided for a House of Chiefs. In all cases the ultimate decision on appeals rests with the Appeal Commissioner sitting with or without assessors.

When any Bill affecting the traditional functions or privileges of a chief is introduced into the National Assembly, the speaker will refer it to the House of Chiefs of the region in which the chief concerned exercises his functions, and no motion shall be moved for the second reading of the Bill in the National Assembly until three months after the date of its introduction into the National Assembly.

The constitution as outlined above went a long way to satisfy the demands of both the chiefs and the Opposition, and its publication was heartily welcomed by all sections of the population. There was at once a dramatic fall in the political barometer of the Gold Coast. Dr. K. A. Busia emphasised his desire to co-operate in making independence a success. The Asantehene called on his people to see that there was peace and harmony in the country, and enjoined those of his subjects who had fled south to come home and settle down peacefully.

The very real fears that March 6th, 1957, might be a day of disturbances instead of a day of rejoicing now evaporated, but there were still some difficulties. Dr. Nkrumah had repeatedly expressed his country's desire

THE NEW GHANA

to remain in the British Commonwealth after gaining its independence, but there was fear that some members of the Commonwealth might oppose the Gold Coast's admission, and thus create an embarrassing situation for Britain. This fear was smothered when on February 21st, 1957, the British Prime Minister announced that the Prime Ministers of the Commonwealth had agreed that Ghana be recognised as a member of the Commonwealth from March 6th, 1957. Ghana was thus to be an independent, sovereign state in the British Commonwealth of Nations, enjoying the same rights and privileges as Britain, Canada, Pakistan, India, Australia, New Zealand, Ceylon and the Union of South Africa. It was a privilege of immense psychological importance.

There was yet another deadlock. It is the sad story of a great people—the Ewe people of Togoland. Their recent history has been one of division and periodic boundary revisions, resulting in the separation of families, tribes and of both from their property.

Germany first secured the territory in Africa through a treaty with an Ewe chief of the village of Togo signed in July 1884, by which the coast between Lome and Port Segouro was put under German protection. The Germans soon pushed into the interior, and further friendly treaties were signed extending their influence throughout Togoland.

In July 1886 a boundary was marked between the British Colony of the Gold Coast and the German territory of Togoland, and in 1890, and later in 1899, the boundary was more clearly defined. By 1904 the final boundary was fixed stretching to the extreme north of the country. As a result, the Dagomba people in the north-centre were divided between the Germans and the British, and in the south the Ewe people of the coastlands were left mainly within the German territory, although about one-fifth of them became members of the British Colony

DEADLOCK!

of the Gold Coast. German Togoland was conquered by Anglo-French forces in August 1914, and during the period of the First World War the Colony was redivided between the French and the British, the French receiving the larger but economically less-developed area. This wartime division was economically unsound and seriously divided the Ewe people, in that about three-fifths came to be under British administration in the Gold Coast, and the rest under French. The Dagombas in the north were put under British rule.

After the First World War yet a third division took place. By the Franco-British Declaration of July 1919, France received about two-thirds of the former German colony, including Lome, the coastline and railways, whilst the British received the poorer, less-developed remainder. This third division made no difference to the Dagombas, but split the Ewes between the French and the British. The British and French mandates were confirmed by the League of Nations in 1922, and from that date onward British Togoland was administered as an integral part of the Gold Coast until, in 1929, the new boundary between the two mandates was finally agreed upon by France and Britain.

The Ewes protested strongly at the National Congress of British West Africa in 1920, and on various other occasions to the League of Nations, but their pleas fell on deaf ears.

The Ewes are an exceptionally strong people, outstanding in physique and intelligence and blessed with the qualities which make for good leadership. They are about one million in number, both French and British, and inhabit an area of roughly 10,000 square miles, split up into three sectors, two under the British and one under the French, the population under each being roughly equal.

The Ewes under the British, as a result of indirect rule, enjoyed some form of local government, but those on the

French side did not enjoy the same degree of freedom. The British educational system, too, was also better liked, and in view of the general preference to conditions under British rule, there has always been considerable movement across the frontier. Moreover, many Ewes on the French side have farms and property in the British zone, tending still further to encourage mass movement, whilst there is considerable traffic in wines, food crops and cocoa over the frontier.

Between 1940 and 1943 the frontier was practically closed by the Vichy Government and this caused the Ewes much concern and dissatisfaction towards the end of the Second World War, resulting in nationalist agitation in both French and British Togoland, aimed at uniting the two territories. The French movement was under an up-and-coming businessman, Mr. Sylvanus Olympio, who was then the head of the British United Africa Company's business in Togoland, whilst the British movement was led by Mr. E. Amu and Mr. Daniel Chapman,[1] both schoolmasters at Achimota College. An All-Ewe Conference was held at Accra in June 1946 at which the need for union was recognised and plans were mooted to effect it. In 1946 both territories were placed under United Nations Trusteeship.

Meanwhile, nationalist agitation was getting more vocal and vehement, and Mr. Olympio went to the United Nations in 1947 and subsequent years, to plead his people's cause. These protests yielded some results. The British and the French, although showing no particular desire for further frontier revisions, agreed that there should be greater co-ordination between the two territories, and to that end initiated measures for freer move-

[1] Mr. Chapman, after service with the United Nations Trusteeship Council, is now Secretary to the Ghana Cabinet and Prime Minister.

DEADLOCK!

ment across the frontier, simpler customs administration and the cessation of double taxation.

The Ewes, still divided, remained far from satisfied, and periodic protests were made to the United Nations. Meanwhile, the Gold Coast was now fast approaching self-government, and in June 1954 Britain informed the United Nations Trusteeship Council that she would not be able to administer British Togoland after the Gold Coast became independent. A United Nations mission was consequently sent to the territory to ascertain the wishes of the population of some 416,000.

The mission, in its report, stated that Togoland had naturally become closely allied with the Gold Coast after forty years of joint administration. The first view favoured integrating Togoland under British administration with the Gold Coast when the latter became independent. The second favoured establishing the identity of Togoland under British administration as a separate unit, preliminary to allowing the people to choose whether to federate with the independent Gold Coast or to unite with an independent Togoland under French administration; the territories so unified to be federated eventually with the independent Gold Coast. All major parties claimed that a plebiscite should be held to decide the future of Togoland, to which the mission agreed. The United Nations accordingly gave its consent.

The British administration in Togoland and the Gold Coast Government under Nkrumah both favoured integration with the Gold Coast, whilst the opposition groups, in particular the National Liberation Movement and the Togoland Congress Party, opted for an independent Togoland which could federate eventually with an independent Gold Coast.

The question of a federal constitution was a highly controversial one. The C.P.P. under Nkrumah maintained that the existence of Togoland as a single unit was not a feasible proposition economically and that the two territories were already so closely associated that to separate them would be an unsound move. Moreover, the interests of the Ewe tribe could be adequately guarded by Gbedemah, himself an Ewe.

The plebiscite was held on May 9th, 1956, under the strict supervision of United Nations observers. The result showed that 93,095 people in the territory voted for union with the Gold Coast, whilst 67,492 people voted for separation, a clear majority of 58 per cent.

The British Government accordingly proposed to the United Nations that the trusteeship should be terminated and that Togoland should be united with the Gold Coast as soon as it achieved independence. This suggestion was finally approved by the United Nations General Assembly in December 1956, and became fact a couple of months later when the Gold Coast became independent.

In this way the Togoland problem was solved. The Dagombas kept intact as part of the independent Gold Coast, and the Ewes remained a divided people.

IX

FROM GOLD COAST TO GHANA

MARCH 6TH, 1957, had been proclaimed as Independence Day, and by the time that all constitutional disputes were settled this date was drawing near. March 6th was chosen because it was the 113th anniversary of the signing of the Bond of 1844, the first major definitive agreement between the British and certain Gold Coast chiefs, who thereby formally acknowledged British rule and agreed to conform to the general pattern of British law and jurisdiction. And now the first British territory in the whole continent of Africa was to become an independent sovereign state within the British Commonwealth.

Some £600,000 were voted by the Government for the celebrations and a number of local celebration committees were formed as well as a national committee, which was set up in Accra, composed of men and women drawn from all walks of life; its Chairman was Kojo Botsio, the Minister of State. The committee was charged with seeing that the day was celebrated in the most fitting manner.

The Government sent invitations to about fifty-six nations, including Britain, the United States of America, the Soviet Union, Communist China, Burma, Ceylon, Canada, Australia, New Zealand, South Africa, Pakistan, India and the independent African states of Tunisia, Liberia and Ethiopia. The continent of South America was represented by delegations, as were Belgium, France and some Eastern European nations. Fernando Po, from which the first cocoa bean had been brought into the country in 1879, was not forgotten.

107

The Government also invited those men and women from all over the world who had in one way or another helped the Gold Coast on its road to independence. Among these were Dr. Ralph Bunehe, the Negro United Nations Expert; Rev. A. G. Fraser, the first principal of Achimota, where the destiny of the future Ghana was determined over thirty years ago; Professor Arthur Lewis of Manchester University, who had advised Nkrumah's Government on its economic programme; Rev. Michael Scott, the champion of the rights of South African Negroes; the late Dr. Jeffreys, the British educational expert; and the late Sir Sidney Abrahams, a former Attorney-General of the Gold Coast. Delegates came from Nigeria, Sierra Leone, Gambia, Kenya, Tanganyika, Uganda, Malaya, British Guiana and the West Indies, whose nationalist interests were akin to those of the Gold Coast.

The status of the leaders of the delegations was evidence of the importance attached to the occasion. America's delegation was led by the Vice-President, Mr. Richard Nixon, who received a tremendous ovation on his arrival; the Soviet Union by a state minister, whilst the British delegation was led by Mr. R. A. Butler, Lord Privy Seal. But the person who was the centre of attraction was the representative of the Queen of the British Commonwealth, H.R.H. The Duchess of Kent.

For the first time since 1925, a British royal visitor had come to West Africa. Fluttering in the sky were the flags of the mother country, Britain, those of the new nation about to be born and those of all other nations represented. At Accra Airport to meet her, on the morning of Saturday, March 2nd, 1957, was the Governor, Sir Charles Arden-Clarke, the Prime Minister, and his Cabinet, the Opposition leaders, members of Parliament, high-ranking Government officials and consuls and representatives of other nations. In addition to these were important chiefs from Ashanti and the other regions, and representatives of various societies and women's organisations, in resplendent attire. The whole airport was transformed into a gigantic panorama of pageantry and pomp. It was a reception befitting a royal visitor. As the Duchess alighted from the B.O.A.C. Stratocruiser which had brought her from Britain, a loud, ear-splitting cheer greeted her spontaneously. A Royal Salute of 21 guns was fired by the 2nd Field Battery, Gold Coast Artillery.

The many Civic welcomes and ceremonies culminated in a state dinner given by the Government at the Ambassador Hotel in Accra on March 4th, at which the Duchess was the guest of honour. About five hundred local and overseas dignitaries, including the heads of the visiting delegations, were present at this impressive gathering, which was made more so by the speeches delivered.

Proposing the toast, the Governor, Sir Charles Arden-Clarke, said the hour of midnight had a magic quality; that traditionally, and certainly in fairy-tales, the hour of midnight was appropriate for the transformation scene. He went on: "And tomorrow by Her Majesty's decree, in this country, at that hour, there will take place a great transformation—the colonial territory of the Gold Coast will become the independent nation of Ghana. By midnight tomorrow this country becomes endowed with the powers, duties and responsibilities of self-government. And at the same time as it takes its place in the comity of nations, it will take its place as a member of a closer brotherhood, the British Commonwealth."

The Governor added that the outward sign of this transformation was the acknowledgment of Her Majesty, the Head of the Commonwealth, as Queen of Ghana. Another visible sign of change, he said, was the presence of the Duchess as Her Majesty's special representative.

Replying to the toast, the Duchess expressed her appreciation of the overwhelming warmth of the reception given her. She stated her disappointment at her inability to visit all regions, and concluded by praising the people's vitality and energy.

Dr. Nkrumah followed. In his speech he expressed the hope that the new state of Ghana would be a centre to which all peoples of Africa might come and where all cultures of Africa would meet. His country's desire was to establish friendly relations with all nations of the world, and it was the desire of Ghana to remain within the British Commonwealth, so long as the member countries sought a solution to common problems by democratic and peaceful methods. He promised help and assistance to British colonial territories at different stages in their march to freedom.

Independence Day was now only a matter of hours away, and already the whole country was in a state of joy and excitement. Late on the night of March 5th, 1957, the Legislative Assembly of the Gold Coast held its last session. It was an historic occasion, for at that last meeting Dr. Nkrumah made a speech which will certainly go down in the history of Ghana as one of the most important he ever made. In a sense, it was the testament of the new nation, whose birth was only an hour off. But it was more than that; it was an expression of the attitude and outlook of colonial people everywhere and of black people in general. Nkrumah dealt with Ghana's association with the Commonwealth, defence and external affairs, trade with other nations, and the interests and advancement of all Africans in pursuit of freedom and social progress. He concluded the great speech as follows:

"Whatever our political differences, whatever our political affiliations or persuasions, let us all unite to work selflessly for the progress and prosperity of our new State of Ghana and her peoples. We have fought and won the battle for freedom. We must now assail the ramparts of all the social and economic evils that have plagued our country all these years, and to win this second battle of economic independence and social reconstruction, I rely on the unqualified support of all sections of the community. Let us march forward together."

X
GHANA IS BORN!

WHEN NKRUMAH finished his speech to a packed House of Members of Parliament, foreign delegates and local dignitaries, it was about seven minutes to the hour of destiny—twelve midnight, March 5th, 1957. Already thousands of people had gathered on the Polo Ground, a large open space a few yards from Parliament House; whilst another huge, excited crowd had gathered round the House itself. They sang and danced, and shouted joyfully: 'Freedom, Freedom, Nkrumah'.

The Union Jack still fluttered over Parliament House until, as midnight struck, it was solemnly lowered and replaced by the red, yellow and green flag of the new state.

With the new flag hoisted, Nkrumah was carried shoulder high to the Polo Ground, where his arrival caused still more excitement and delight. Little wonder that the Prime Minister broke down in emotion in those early hours of March 6th, 1957. As he wept for joy and danced, waving his handkerchief, the masses realised fully that independence had come.

With his departure many of the crowd, estimated at over 90,000, dispersed, but the rest remained to dance, chatter and sing until well into the morning of March 6th, 1957.

The climax of the Independence Day celebrations was the State Opening of Parliament by the Duchess of Kent. Hours before the event, thousands of people had gathered round Parliament House. Banners and flags decorated the route from Government House to Parliament House,

GHANA IS BORN!

where the Members of Parliament, the official delegates and invited guests, and a battery of foreign correspondents and Pressmen waited.

Amid shouting, singing and cheering, Nkrumah arrived in a Rolls-Royce. The enthusiasm of the people to shake hands with their leader was overwhelming and only skilled effort on the part of the police prevented his being carried shoulder high by the crowd into Parliament House.

Next to arrive was the Governor, Sir Charles Arden-Clarke, the man who had done so much to make the nation's longing a reality. Looking resplendent in his official regalia, Sir Charles was obviously satisfied with the great ovation which greeted him, the last British Governor. Sir Charles was ushered into the House and sworn in as the first Governor-General of the new nation of Ghana. His frank, sincere speech at the ceremony was the consummation of the thoughts and experiences of a typical British Colonial Servant and great administrator.

As the Governor-General was being sworn in, the Duchess's drive from Government House began, heralded by a 21-gun salute fired by the 2nd Field Battery, Ghana Artillery, and followed by a 21-gun salute by Her Majesty's ships and a ship of the Pakistan Navy, anchored in Accra Roads. All along the route the Duchess received a loud ovation from the crowd. Royal Air Force Valiants and Royal Australian Air Force Neptunes flew over her carriage, which was escorted by a mounted troop of the Ghana police and by contingents of the Armed Services. On arrival at the Parliament of Ghana, the Duchess was received by the new Governor-General, given the Royal Salute and led into the House by the Speaker's procession, while a fanfare was sounded.

The Duchess met a very animated House, with the M.P.s in their gorgeous Kente Cloths and the Visitors' Galleries packed. Dressed in a full-length white dress radiant with diamonds, her tiara and necklace glittered even in the light of the day, as gracefully she moved to take the throne. The legal papers under which the Duchess was empowered by the Queen to open Ghana's first Parliament on her behalf, were read by the Clerk and Nkrumah then presented the Queen's speech to the Duchess, which she delivered from the throne.

Her Majesty regretted that she could not be present herself 'on the occasion of the opening of the first session of the Parliament of Ghana'. The Queen went on to review the course of history which led to a time when 'Less than a month ago I gave my assent to the Ghana Independence Act'. She outlined the principal constitutional changes in the relations between Ghana and the mother country and also Britain's intentions for the future, and concluded with a personal message to the people:

> I have entrusted to my Aunt the duty of opening, on my behalf, the first session of the Parliament of Ghana.
>
> My thoughts are with you on this great day as you take up the full responsibilities of independent nationhood, and I rejoice to welcome another new member of our growing commonwealth family of nations.
>
> The hopes of many, especially in Africa, hang on your endeavours.
>
> It is my earnest and confident belief that my people in Ghana will go forward in freedom and justice, in unity among themselves and in brotherhood with all the peoples of the Commonwealth.
>
> May God bless you all.

Nor were the celebrations confined only to Ghana. In London, although the rain poured down on that March 6th, big crowds with umbrellas gathered to watch the hoisting of the Ghana flag from the Ghana office; and the band of the Welsh Guards played a Ghanaian hymn of praise during the ceremony. Flag-hoisting ceremonies in many towns were performed by Ghana communities and

GHANA IS BORN!

friends, and a state dinner was given in London by the Ghana Commissioner to mark the occasion. Leading British statesmen and officers, including the Prime Minister, Mr. Harold Macmillan, were present.

In a special broadcast message to the people of Britain during the night of March 6th, Mr. Macmillan said that Britain wished Ghana well in the great task before her and would give her 'all the help we can'. He hoped for a 'long and happy association with us and our partners as members of this great Commonwealth of Nations'. Mr. Macmillan continued:

> We have had a very long connection with the Gold Coast as traders, as missionaries and as administrators. Today we see the fruition of a long effort, to which British men and women have made a great contribution.
>
> Now the five million people of the Gold Coast have become self-governing and independent. They have prepared for this by their own efforts and have equipped themselves with our help and guidance, to shoulder the heavy responsibilities of full nationhood.
>
> This is a great day for them and I want you to feel that it is a great day for us, for it marks the success of what we set our hands to achieve.
>
> The first act they have taken as an independent government is to seek admission to the Commonwealth and to retain their loyalty to the Queen.
>
> We rejoice, too, that Ghana has chosen the path of parliamentary democracy and has accepted our political values.
>
> Dr. Nkrumah has demonstrated his belief in these principles by accepting a constitution especially devised to meet the needs and anxieties of the peoples of Ashanti and the Northern Territories.

Britain's pride on that historic day was more than justified, for it had led, patiently and calmly, a collection of warring, divided tribes and states for 113 years, to make out of them a progressive, modern African nation. It was an achievement second to none in the world's colonial history and a challenge to other colonial powers.

Less than twenty-four hours after the new state had come into being, Dr. Nkrumah's Government applied for membership of the United Nations, being sponsored by all the nations of the British Commonwealth, with the exception of South Africa. The Security Council quickly approved Ghana's application, which was then put before the General Assembly, who, by a unanimous vote, admitted Ghana as the eighty-first member. Thus Ghana was established in the brotherhood of nations.

XI

AFTER MARCH 6TH—WHAT NEXT

GHANA'S FREEDOM is now a matter of history. The question which intelligent people in the country and abroad have been asking is: 'After March 6th—what next?' What is going to happen in the young state? Can it uphold the principles and concepts of democracy and freedom which were reaffirmed at its birth? Will it live on to be a beacon to other African states or degenerate into a barbaric, third-class nation? Answers to these questions are urgently needed.

It is unfair to assess a Government's progress so soon. The new Government has not been in power long enough for an accurate review of its success or failure on the home front to be made, and it is not proposed here to undertake such a task. However, two or three recent incidents of great significance must be mentioned.

The first of these is the disturbances which took place in the Trans-Volta-Togoland Region during the independence celebrations. The causes of these disturbances were purely political, and were due to the dissatisfaction which some groups in the southern part of Togoland felt at the incorporation of Togoland into Ghana, an event which had been the express wish of the majority of the people and which conformed with the decisions of the United Nations General Assembly. The disgruntled ones would not allow the rest of the population to join in the celebrations, and went about pulling down the flags, banners and bunting put up by the Government.

Under the influence of the inflamed oratory of certain leaders, the people refused to heed persistent Government

with the police
had to be sent
ctive measures
y that it was
irbance.

Government's
in mind, how-
e allowed full
ere is strong
d by further,
ina can learn
n by internal
is the royal
outing of its
laws. The world will watch with interest to see how Ghana can maintain law and order by democratic means.

The presence of Dr. Nkrumah at the July 1957 Conference of the British Commonwealth Prime Ministers in London was an event of great significance to the coloured peoples of the world and to Ghana in particular. For the first time an African Prime Minister was sitting, on equal terms, in conference with leaders from Asia, America and Australasia, discussing world problems. This was the concrete, visible expression of the independence of a new nation. That Dr. Nkrumah openly and clearly answered all Press criticisms, and even went to the extent of writing an article in a British paper to clear his Government of certain allegations which were current in his country and in Britain, is a definite indication that he is still committed to the principles of fair deal, democracy and freedom, which were reaffirmed at Ghana's birth. He desires still to hold on to Britain's friendship and goodwill.

It is obvious that Dr. Nkrumah fully realises that the success or failure of Ghana as a nation will determine to a large extent the fate of other colonial territories. Speaking to excited crowds which welcomed him back to Accra

AFTER MARCH 6TH—WHAT NEXT?

on his return from London, Dr. Nkrumah said: "We have got to build Ghana into a stable independent country—an example for other African countries. We have been asked to demonstrate to the outside world that the African, once given the chance, can stand on his own."

On the economic front the new state faces considerable difficulties. Dr. Nkrumah has ordered a brief interim period of rest and consolidation before plunging into the second Five-year Development Programme; a wise measure, for there is much national stocktaking to be done. Political independence is impossible without economic freedom and stability. "I ask you to keep up the same spirit which led us to independence. This will help our bid for peace and comfort. We will make Ghana a showpiece of the continent of Africa. And I have brought back with me the plan for achieving this." With these words Nkrumah greeted his enthusiastic countrymen on his return from London in July 1957. They show a realisation of the importance and seriousness of the fight on the economic front.

Nkrumah's plan has not yet begun to unfold, and the people in the meantime are crying out for more houses and more jobs. If Nkrumah is able to apply the same enthusiasm and ability that he brought to bear in solving his people's political problems, his name will go down in history as a great politician and outstanding statesman.

But all is not well in the new state. The fears of many outsiders that the withdrawal of British rule might result in the re-emergence of tribal wars, petty jealousies and regional factions seem to be coming true, a state of affairs that would not commend itself to democratically minded people anywhere, least of all in Ghana, with March 6th, 1957, still so vividly in mind. There is no doubt that it was British rule principally which carved out of warring tribes a modern, united state. There is the tendency for a young nation, psychologically used to a century and more of foreign rule by a people of different colour, creed and outlook, not to accord to its own Government the respect and honour which it would readily accord foreign rulers.

Already there are clear signs that these tribal differences and jealousies tend to become political in character, with the result that political parties are formed based on these rifts; if this trend continues it is likely that within a decade or two, tribal wars will have broken out once more. Parties whose strength is derived from religion or tribal feelings will in the long run do a nation—especially a young nation like Ghana—much harm, as it could mean only one thing—that the African when left to his own devices is unable to rule himself. It is the duty of the Government during the initial stage of a nation's life to forestall such a situation arising by educating public opinion.

That great friend and admirer of the Ghana people, Sir Charles Arden-Clarke, went home in May 1957. After eight hectic years in West Africa he was able to describe himself as being 'the best cheered Governor'; a statement much in contrast with one he made almost eight years previously, that he was 'the best booed Governor'. The gifts showered on him by the people during his farewell tour, and the fine sentiments of friendship and goodwill expressed, showed how grateful everyone felt to Sir Charles Arden-Clarke for his careful guidance in those eight years. Again the people's respect and desire for closer friendship with the mother country, Great Britain, was repeatedly stated. Sir Charles's administration had shown them the best element in British colonial rule, but what was more, it had demonstrated Britain's goodwill and interest in her former colonial territory.

No wonder, then, that the announcement in June 1957 of the appointment of a Labour peer, the Earl of Listowel, to be the nation's next Governor-General, was

AFTER MARCH 6TH—WHAT NEXT?

heartily acclaimed by all sections of the Ghana Press and public. If the achievement of Sir Charles Arden-Clarke is anything to go by, the people's joy over this appointment is entirely justified.

In an historic interview with the world Press in Accra on the day following Independence, the Prime Minister, Dr. Nkrumah, in an answer to a question about the appointment of the next Governor-General after Sir Charles, had stated that for the next two years at least, for political reasons, a Briton would hold the post, and only after that time would the appointment of an African be considered. Nkrumah has kept his promise like a gentleman. And although, until the Earl of Listowel arrived, an eminent African, of great public respect and brilliance, the Chief Justice, Sir Arku Korsah, acted as Governor-General and did remarkably well, holding his high office to the satisfaction of all the regions, it is prudent that for a while the country take Nkrumah's advice.

Finally, the problem of the effects of March 6th, 1957, on the world at large may be considered. That the independence of Ghana was bound to resurrect demands of other colonial territories to ask for greater freedom and justice was abundantly clear to the more politically alert all over the world. This influence of Ghana's liberation is going to be seriously felt, particularly among the colonial peoples in Africa. Just as five years before Nkrumah and his supporters in the Gold Coast, looking at Liberia, its economic stability and political system, had convinced themselves that the Gold Coast could also flourish on its own, so the independence of Ghana would prompt many other Africans to ask: 'If Ghana, why not us also?' They demand an answer.

African nationalism was awakened long before March 6th, 1957, and Ghana's independence has encouraged the demands of African nationalists to be more vocal and determined. The spirit of nationalism is at work, though these demands do not necessarily suggest that foreign domination is an evil or a selfish thing. They are merely an expression of the pent-up, nationalistic feelings of peoples who now 'prefer self-government with danger to servitude in tranquillity'.

In South Africa, Central Africa, Uganda, Kenya, Tanganyika, the West Indies and British West Africa, African peoples and descendants of Africans rejoiced on March 6th about Ghana's independence. They were jubilant because they felt that the freedom of Ghana was in measure the liberation of all colonial territories. It has given them new hope, for it means the recognition of African people by the white races of the world.

It is likely that March 6th [1] will have direct political and constitutional benefits to these territories, for the colonial powers will have to find an answer, willy-nilly, to nationalists' questions and demands. The clock of progress cannot be put back. Other colonial powers might bear in mind the degree of co-operation, understanding and judgment shown in the evolution of Ghana.

What has taken place in Ghana is only a repetition of what has already happened in Asia. After India and Pakistan, it was the turn of Burma, to be followed quickly by Ceylon. After Ceylon, it was Ghana's turn, and after Ghana, it will be Malaya. Out of a conglomeration of subject peoples, Britain is creating a mammoth association of friendly, independent nations, bound together by goodwill, common desire for peace, democracy and freedom, and with a common purpose and faith.

---

[1] March 6th, 1957, was also noteworthy as the day on which a book was published which will undoubtedly have great influence on the thoughts and actions of nationalist leaders in other parts of Africa. *Ghana*, the autobiography of Kwame Nkrumah, will be an inspiration to other African leaders, and to a considerable extent mould their policies, actions and plans.

XII

PROBLEMS OF INDEPENDENCE

GHANA HAS won its independence, but the problems which the country inevitably has to face are far more serious than the initial achievement of freedom. The qualities of the country's leaders have been put to the test and, judging from the results, they have acquitted themselves well. They have done what they set out to achieve —no mean feat. It is fitting, therefore, that the world should accord to them the congratulation they so much deserve, although we must not forget that Nkrumah's predecessors, notably Dr. Danquah, have helped to pave the way to freedom. The subsequent and by far the most acid test of leadership and statecraft, which had its beginnings on March 6th, 1957, is yet to come.

It would be well to consider some of the many problems which still confront Dr. Nkrumah and his Government:

1. *Agriculture*

Ghana is primarily an agricultural country and is likely to remain so for many years to come. With such rapid world progress, however, the time has come when closer attention should be paid to the country's agricultural future. The cocoa crop is the foundation-stone of Ghana's economy, and about 70 per cent of Ghana's revenue is derived from the industry. At the moment, the crop is yielded by small-scale peasant farmers, using ancient and trusted methods—the scratching of the ground with the hoe, the hand-picking of the harvest. The processes are slow, tiring, and the results obtained are quite out of proportion to the amount of labour involved. It is in the industry's own interests that modern large-scale farming should replace as soon as possible this out-of-date system. Naturally enough, opposition would be met from the farmers themselves, and this is only to be expected; but it can be circumvented by an extensive programme throughout the country, designed to introduce to the farmers the advantages of the new methods and to convince them that their own future is at stake. With improved methods of growing, cultivation, harvesting and drying, the cocoa farms could be made to yield larger crops with the same amount of labour. Such a programme would result in considerable expenditure—for travelling, transport and literature—but an expenditure which would be worth its weight in gold. Without such a programme, the cocoa crop will soon be insufficient to meet world demands. As a result of a recent amendment to earlier legislation, the funds derived from cocoa, which are kept on behalf of the farmers by the Cocoa Marketing Board, are being used to finance minor projects of local importance in all regions, including the north, which does not produce cocoa but which is the main source of labour employed on the farms.

The present efforts to check and control the Swollen Shoot disease must be maintained and, in addition, substantial funds must be voted to the West African Research Institute at Tafo and, where necessary, other centres abroad, to undertake extensive research in strains and varieties of cocoa which are more resistant to Swollen Shoot and other diseases to which the cocoa tree is prone. Research into varieties of cocoa which bear heavier crops easily and quickly is another field which could be of wonderful benefit to the country.

It is paradoxical that the cocoa crop, so important to the country's economy, offers no possibilities of becoming part of the staple diet, despite the Government's efforts to make it so by lowering duties on imported cocoa products. The main food crops are maize, millet, rice, plantains, cassava, yams, cocoyams, groundnuts and pulses, but here again the yield per acre is negligible in comparison with the amount of work involved, added to which transport facilities from the rural areas to the main centres of population are quite inadequate, resulting occasionally in food shortages in the larger towns whilst the crops rot and spoil in the bush. If Ghana is not to become dependent upon imported foods, there must be widespread expansion in the cultivation of these food crops, and in view of the ample scope for development in agriculture, this should be possible. Already much of the nation's rice is imported, whilst the potentialities of large-scale rice production in the Nzima area have not been seriously considered.

The Government is advised by a National Food Board on measures to encourage food production, whilst some evolutionary schemes are worked out by the Agricultural Development Corporation and the Gonja Development Company. The importance of producing food crops, abundantly and at the appropriate places, cannot be over-emphasised, for as history has proved time and time again, when a nation's stomach is empty for long revolution follows.

Malnutrition is one of the greatest causes of infant mortality in Ghana. The local diet is chiefly carbohydrate, with an extremely low protein content. This deficiency in proteins is made up by imported meat and fish, though an effort should be made to render the country less dependent on these two imports by means of greater home production. In 1955 alone the country paid £13 million for imported meat and dairy products, wheat flour, sugar and fish, this sum constituting about 15 per cent of the total value of imports. The Government is making efforts to improve farming, through the use of up-to-date methods and by soil and water conservation (though here considerable difficulty is met through lack of water and the incidence of disease) and fishing, by the introduction of motor-boats and the modernising of fishermen's ideas.

The country's efforts to produce other cash crops in addition to cocoa should be more seriously pursued. Other nations are now beginning to show interest in the production of cocoa, and the Swollen Shoot disease in Ghana makes the whole future of the industry unpredictable. At present, apart from cocoa, there is very little export of crops. Those that are exported are mostly cola, coffee, cotton and fibres, palm-kernels and some fruits.

The agricultural system, then, poses gigantic problems for Dr. Nkrumah's Government, and its efforts to develop major cash crops are still chiefly in the experimental stage. But without agriculture Ghana could not exist.

2. *Mining and Industrialisation*

Ghana's chief mineral resources are gold, diamonds, manganese and bauxite. Although the miners are not producing the main source of national revenue, their importance has been rising considerably in recent years. However, gold mining has been seriously hampered of late by the fixed world gold price and by rising costs and labour unrest. A few mines have had to close down, and the Government, in order to prevent further financial collapse, has given tax and financial relief to some of them.

The absence of coal and iron in the country has made it difficult to embark upon any serious programme for industry, much as the Government would like to do so. Coupled with this is the shortage of trained personnel for executive and managerial duties and of skilled workmen and artisans. If the Government is to surmount these formidable problems and make Ghana the paradise the politicians promised and the local inhabitants anxiously await, considerable foreign capital will be required, which will not be forthcoming unless foreign capitalists are assured of the country's stability economically and politically.

As a start, the Government, through the Industrial Development Corporation, is gradually introducing the people to small-scale industry, and helping them by way of finance and advice. Repeated major policy statements by Dr. Nkrumah in Parliament and abroad give abundant proof of the Government's realisation of the need for foreign capital and its desire to ensure its safety. Although the Government claims to be Socialist, it has no intention of nationalising foreign concerns, and the constitution of 1957 explicitly guarantees appropriate compensations in the event of any future nationalisation.

The Volta River Project offers the greatest hopes for industry, but the financial provisions have yet to be worked out and final decisions have not been taken by Nkrumah's Government. The Prime Minister is personally interested in getting the scheme going as soon as possible, and recent utterances from political sources suggest that a way will be found.

If the Volta River Project goes through successfully, it will go a long way to solving Ghana's economic problems. With the same impatience that characterised their demand for independence from Britain, Ghanaians are now pressing their own people for jobs. It would appear, however, that only an expanded agriculture and some degree of industrialisation, plus the Volta Project, can provide an answer.

3. *National Identity*

With the release from British rule there is a tendency for suspicion and mistrust, based on purely tribal feelings, to flare up once more. The northerners fear that the south may exploit their ignorance and general backwardness;

whilst the Ashantis still remember the history of their ancient kingdom when they held dominion over many other tribes and states. The age-old fear of the Fantis still persists among the Ashantis.

Only a feeling of national identity can completely suppress these tendencies, and the people should be made to think of themselves as citizens of Ghana, rather than as members of different tribes. This is no easy task, but much could be done in this direction by the Social Welfare Department and Information Services, given adequate funds, by means of films, leaflets in the vernacular, oral classes and discussions. The people need to be educated to the realisation that under the Constitution of March 6th, 1957, they are all one, that there is no difference between a Fanti, Ga, Ashanti, Hausa or Ewe. In this direction the Convention People's Party has done well to appeal to the people's national feelings and not to their innate parochial sentiments. Other political groups might profitably follow their lead, and not capitalise on the masses' tendency to think in terms of tribe or region.

The primary and secondary schools present a fertile field in which the feeling of national spirit can be instilled. Children, from toddlers upwards, should be taught to think and act as members of one nation, as citizens of Ghana, imbued with respect and love for their country, their country's flag and its national anthem. These are measures which, in a nation so young, cannot but be recommended. Liberia, the oldest independent African state in West Africa, has something to teach Ghana in this respect, for in every primary school [1] 'toddlers snap to attention every morning, assembled for the hoist, to pledge their allegiance to the Flag and to the Republic for which it stands; one nation indivisible, with liberty and justice for all'.

[1] Published speech by Liberian Consul in Accra on Liberian Independence Day.

PROBLEMS OF INDEPENDENCE

The principal, visible characteristics of tribal differentiation—the tribal marks on the face—should be strongly discouraged by every possible means. This ancient custom of marking the faces of newly born infants with the particular pattern or sign of their tribes no longer serves any purpose. In the old days of inter-tribal wars and slavery, these marks made it easy to identify tribal casualties and distinguish aliens. It is doubtful if there are any medical grounds to sustain the custom, which now serves principally to heighten tribal consciousness and disfigure the faces of unfortunate babies! The custom is gradually becoming less fashionable, particularly among the more educated, but it is by no means extinct.

On the other hand, tribal inter-marriage should be encouraged as much as possible by persuasion, argument and mass-education. Only by the intermingling of tribes both at work and off duty, so that they can learn each other's languages, customs and habits and realise that the fate of their country hangs upon their co-operation one with the other, can the advantages of such marriages be brought home to all.

There is also an urgent need for a lingua-franca, and if it is to serve any useful national purpose, it must be Twi, the language of the majority of Ghanaians. English will still remain the official language, however, and the common link between the different tribes and communities.

Much could also be done by the Broadcasting Department and Information Services and the new Ministry of Information and Broadcasting under that firm, level-headed, young socialist, Mr. Kofi Baako, to educate the masses and give them pride in their great nation.

4. *Education and Social Amenities*

The greatest achievement of the present Government, since it came into power in 1951, has been in the field of education. Within a few years the numbers of pupils in elementary and secondary schools have more than doubled, whilst there has been a tremendous increase in the number of teachers under training throughout the country. In the towns and villages there are hundreds of schools, sometimes uncongenially housed, but without doubt doing a great job of educating thousands of African children, who would otherwise have remained untutored. But a lot still remains to be done. The people are crying out for more and more schools for their children. If the Government can maintain the present pace in its educational programme, there is every prospect that within a decade or so Ghana will emerge as an enlightened, educated nation.

With the achievement of independence, it becomes imperative that the education of the whole nation be modified to suit Ghana's new status. Schoolchildren should be reading books written by Africans, books designed to imbue them with a feeling of national respect and the desire to serve the nation, apart from fulfilling all the requirements expected of any educational programme. They must be taught more about Ghana, its ancient and modern history, its handicaps and difficulties and of the men and women, such as Okomfo Anokye, the great Ashantihenes, Sarbah, Asamani, Ato-Ahumah and Dr. Aggrey, who have helped to give it the status it enjoys today.

The provision of more secondary and technical schools and institutions is another problem which faces the Government. This has resulted mainly from the large increase in elementary schools during the last few years. Emphasis, at this stage in Ghana's development, on technical education is very important, as numbers of the older generation have for some reason the idea fixed in their minds that even skilled technical work and large-scale farming are not proper occupations for literate people. There are not enough white-collar jobs to go round, and if the hundreds of school lads leaving the primary and secondary schools are not to become loafers and vagabonds, they would be advised, and should be encouraged, to learn the science of farming or a skilled trade.

Recent statements about this problem by many labour officers and some ministers, particularly Mr. Kojo Botsio and Mr. Kofi Baako, are in the right direction, but there is a long way to go.

In the field of mass-education, the Social Welfare Department has, within a short time, made great strides in training thousands of adults to read and write their own vernaculars, and much of the credit must go to Mr. R. K. Gardiner, until recently head of the department. The illiterate masses are gradually being introduced to modern concepts of hygiene and decent living. Opportunity is made, through discussion and classes on Ghana, to explain to them the need for paying taxes and leading a life of self-sacrifice and self-help. An understanding of their country's economic foundations and stability and the problems which their leaders have to face will also help them to realise how far the Government can meet all their demands for houses, jobs, more food, cheap consumer goods and low taxes.

5. *Housing and Health*

Throughout the country the housing problem is acute, and the people are emphatically demanding more and better houses in which to live. The Government's progress in this sphere is relatively small compared with the strides it has taken in the field of education and the provision of roads and general works. A series of costly experiments have not produced the results hoped for, and the successive changes in the Government's housing policy are ample proof of the difficulties encountered and the efforts to solve them.

The rickety huts in which the villagers live and the

overcrowded, unwholesome houses in the towns cannot but lead to general ill health and the spread of disease. The problem can only be solved by the Government with the co-operation of private enterprise.

The Minister of Housing has recently made promises to build houses, both for letting and for sale, for the working classes and also for clerks, teachers, nurses and others in a higher income group, to clear the slums and to re-develop the towns and villages. These changes are essential in order to give Ghana a new lease of life in this sphere, and to put them into effect will require all the planning acumen, foresight, personnel and funds that the Government can muster without dislocating seriously the general development programme for the country.

Closely connected with the housing problem is the equally serious one of health. In spite of the Government's laudable efforts since 1951 to provide hospital facilities in most of the principal towns and a host of clinics and dispensaries in the villages and remote districts, the health of the nation as a whole is far from good, and it is particularly poor in the north.

The first solution, apart from adequate medical facilities, would be the provision to as many people as possible of a pipe-borne water supply. The present situation is a vicious circle. Apart from malaria, leprosy and one or two other skin diseases, and venereal disease which has not hitherto been a serious threat but which is now becoming rampant, most of the diseases are due to contaminated water. Through ignorance and the lack of fresh water the people drink the dirty, muddy filth from the streams, rivers and pools, and it is little wonder that they become stricken with dysentery, typhoid, bilharziasis, tuberculosis and guinea-worms. The few doctors available treat and cure them, whence they go back to the villages and towns, drink the same water and become stricken with the disease yet again!

Much could be done by the information services, the Social Welfare Department (which has already begun the task) and the Ministry of Information and Broadcasting to explain to the people the need for personal hygiene and of drinking fresh water; but, nevertheless, if there is no fresh water on hand, the people are bound to resort to their former unhealthy supply. The need for piped water is an essential.

Apart, however, from these problems, one of the most serious menaces to the nation's health is the dearth of doctors. There are, at the present time, 206 doctors to cater for a population of about five million—an average of one doctor to every 25,000 people. Even if the present supply of doctors is maintained, it will take at least eighty years before the country can boast of having enough. Until that time, malnutrition and disease will continue to take their toll of the lives of the Ghanaians.

The future is undoubtedly bleak, though one cannot but admire the present efforts of the Government. The number of scholarships for medical studies abroad is steadily increasing, whilst the possibility of establishing in the near future a medical faculty at the University College of Ghana is being seriously considered.

These problems are not new; they were in existence long before March 6th, 1957, but just as the people pressed their right to independence, so now they demand a solution from Nkrumah and his Government to these more personal problems. The eyes of the world rest on him to see how he will cope with them.

XIII

UNANSWERED QUESTIONS

THE DEMOCRATIC state of Ghana poses serious questions, not only for West Africans but for others also who have not yet attained self-rule. The answers to these questions will in some measure either confirm the opinions held by non-Africans about Africans or act as a challenge. Consideration must be given to a few of these questions, which the more serious-minded sections of the population in Ghana, and to a certain extent the outside world, are beginning to ask, although there can be no definite answers to them.

1. *Can Democracy thrive in Ghana?*

The Government and the Opposition both claim to want a democratic state, but public statements are not enough. There is a need for confirmation by definite action. If democracy is to thrive in Ghana there must be greater respect and sympathy for the opinions and views of the minority, however distasteful these may be, so that ultimately the best policy can be worked out for the whole country and not for just a particular section.

The Government's recent steps to set up a special scholarship fund for students from Northern Ghana is a move in the right direction which, apart from helping to further education in an area which is relatively backward, will also help convince the northerners that the southern majority have their interests at heart.

The temptation is great, indeed, in a young nation like Ghana, for the party in power, if it has a large majority in the Legislature, to bulldoze its measures through the

House irrespective of the views of the minority, and it behoves the Government to move cautiously. It should also take the Opposition more into its confidence, and so achieve a greater measure of co-operation to the common good.

An equally serious temptation in an underdeveloped country is for the Opposition to fall into a state of complacency and automatically take an opposite line to that of the Government on all occasions. An Opposition, as the watchdog of the rights of the minority, should offer a feasible alternative programme—and therein lies the hope for democracy in Ghana—not merely aim to exhibit the loopholes and weaknesses of their opponents' plans.

The present constitution is democratically inspired and needs to be worked in a spirit of mutual trust and confidence.

2. *Will Ghana revert to Tribal Barbarism?*

The removal of British rule from Ghana makes it important to consider this question, for there is no doubt that the cohesive force between the hitherto warring tribes was British influence and British arms. Reversion to tribal barbarism and feuds could be only too easy if adequate precautions are not taken.

Firm foundations, laid by the British both in the Civil Service and the judiciary, should militate against such tendencies, but the danger is there. Too many people think in terms of tribe or region. Inter-tribal jealousies, long buried, have lately begun to reappear, mainly due to the action of smart local politicians ready to exploit them to their own advantage. These local parties and their rulers should appeal to people's national sentiments, not to their selfish, parochial interests, and their aim should be to win confidence and votes on these lines. Similarly, the Government, by mass-education as well as by its own actions, should convince the population that there is no distinction between religions, classes, tribes or families.

The instance is often quoted of Indonesia, a coloured nation, which put up the flags a few years ago only to revert to internal feuds and battles. It rests on the shoulders of the present leaders of Ghana to see that their country does not suffer a similar fate.

3. *After Nkrumah—What Next?*

Long before Independence Day it was apparent that Nkrumah was the one force capable of exerting the same binding influence as the British, and since March 6th, 1957, this has been abundantly proved. Nkrumah is a national figure not just a political leader, a man acclaimed by all sides. Opposition charges of bribery and corruption, nepotism and jobbery, are directed at some of his ministers and followers, but never at Nkrumah himself. Nkrumah's position in contemporary Ghana may be compared with that of Sir Winston Churchill in Britain during the last war, and to some extent with that of Pandit Nehru in present-day India.

For the sake of peace and order, both in the national interest as well as in that of the C.P.P., it is sincerely to be hoped that Nkrumah may be spared to exert his influence on the political scene for a long time to come.

4. *Will Ghana leave the Commonwealth?*

Ghana's membership of the British Commonwealth of Nations is explicitly stated in the constitution of 1957, and major policy statements by both Dr. Nkrumah and by Dr. K. A. Busia always confirm their respective wishes that this should continue.

Historical, sentimental and economic reasons should compel Ghana to remain in the Commonwealth. In the present world state small nations like Ghana cannot, for military reasons, afford to isolate themselves in a watertight compartment of neutrality. They must associate with greater world powers, and the British Commonwealth of Nations offers just such an association.

Writing in the highly esteemed quarterly magazine, *Foreign Affairs*, Mr. Habib Bourguiba, President of Tunisia and founder of Tunisia's independence movement, says history proves that unilateral declarations of neutrality and even non-aggression pacts fail to stand up in the face of large-scale conflict, and that the greatest security offered small nations is solidarity. Young nations, Mr. Bourguiba maintains, must first of all assure themselves of protection against aggression, and he feels that for any single one of them partnership in a collective security system is usually a sufficient guarantee of security.

Ghana's position in world affairs is akin to that of Tunisia, and its leaders realise the helplessness of their country in a divided world.

It is possible that within the next five years Ghana may become a republic, and should that happen the odds are strongly in favour of its remaining within the Commonwealth. In so doing, it would only be following the examples set by Pakistan and Ceylon.

"If the country were to force me to establish Ghana as a republic, I will go with them to that extent. But I think most certainly that it will be within the Commonwealth as is the case in India." Dr. Nkrumah was replying to questions about the possibility of Ghana becoming a republic at a Press conference at Accra the day after Independence Day.

5. *Will Ghana Succeed?*

If the lofty sentiments expressed by local and foreign leaders in Accra on Ghana's independence are of any significance, then it behoves the people of Ghana to make a success of the experiment in African democracy which they have begun.

And here it is only right to reiterate that Ghana has a moral duty to try, and try hard, for the sake of other colonial peoples whose demands for freedom could but be strengthened and justified. But will Ghana succeed? It is a question which no one can answer, not even Nkrumah or Busia. Only Time can tell.

APPENDIX A

Statistical Tables

Table 1. *Area, Population, etc.*

Area in Sq. Miles	Population	Exports	Imports	No. of School-children
		1945		
91,843	3,700,000	£15,743,607	£10,954,187	198,000
		1950–1		
91,843	4,112,000	£91,249,000	£63,313,000	280,000
		1955		
91,843	4,620,000	£96,000,000	£87,000,000	559,000

Table 2. *Population of Principal Towns* [1]

Accra	200,000
Kumasi	78,000
Sekondi-Takoradi	60,000
Cape Coast	57,000
Koforidua	23,000
Tamale	17,000

[1] *Ghana: A Brief Political and Economic Survey* (Royal Institute of International Affairs, May 1957); *Ghana Weekly Review* (Ghana Government, March 1957).

THE NEW GHANA

Table 3. *Direction of Trade*[1]

	Imports (*per cent.*)			Exports (*per cent.*)		
	1953	1954	1955	1953	1954	1955
Great Britain . .	55	49	47	42	40	41
Other Sterling Areas `	5	6	7	4	4	6
Netherlands . .	8	8	8	6	10	11
Western Germany .	3	5	5	7	14	12
Other OEEC Countries . .	12	14	12	9	7	8
United States . .	5	4	4	27	17	18
Canada . . .	1	2	1	1	0·4	0·4
Other Dollar Areas .	0·1	0·4	1	—	—	—
Japan . . .	6	7	10	—	—	—
Totals .	95	95	95	96	92	96

Table 4. *Revenue and Expenditure* (*in £ million sterling*)[1]

	1950–1	1953–4	1954–5
Current Revenue:			
Cocoa Duty . . .	9·1	18·8	20·6
Direct Taxation . .	4·5	5·7	5·2
Other	11·8	21·9	24·9
Totals . .	25·4	46·4	50·7
Current Expenditure . .	12·4	25·1	34·0
Current Surplus . . .	13·0	21·3	16·7
Totals . .	25·4	46·4	50·7

[1] *Ghana: A Brief Political and Economic Survey* (Royal Institute of International Affairs, May 1957).

APPENDIX B

Dates of Important Events

1482: First European Settlement, by the Portuguese.
1844 (March 6th): Bond signed between Britain and some Fanti chiefs. Beginning of British rule in Ghana.
1896: British occupied Kumasi and declared Ashanti a Protectorate.
1901: Ashanti annexed as a Crown Colony.
Northern Territories declared a Protectorate and annexed.
1925: Formation of Provincial Councils.
1919–27: Administration of Gold Coast by Sir Gordon Guggisberg resulted in improvement of medical facilities, education; opening of Achimota College, Takoradi Harbour.
1946: Introduction of 'Burns Constitution' gave the country considerable African majority in Legislative Council; unified the regions of the Gold Coast.
1947: Formation of the United Gold Coast Convention by Dr. J. B. Danquah.
1948: Riots and disturbances in the Gold Coast. A Royal Commission, under Mr. A. K. Watson investigated causes of disturbances.
1949: Coussey Committee sat and produced a constitution giving substantial self-rule to the country.
Nkrumah formed the Convention People's Party in June.
Sir Charles Arden-Clarke arrived as Governor.
1950: Nkrumah declared nation-wide strike in the Gold Coast; arrested with eight others and jailed.

APPENDIX B

1951: Coussey Constitution came into effect. First General Elections won by the C.P.P.
Nkrumah released from prison to head the new Government.

1952: Nkrumah made first Prime Minister; thus becoming the first African in any British dependency to hold such office.

1954: New Constitution introduced, virtually granting self-government. Second General Elections won by the C.P.P.
National Liberation movement (N.L.M.) formed in Ashanti, by Baffuor Osei Okoto. Offered strong opposition to C.P.P.

1956: Alterations to 1954 Constitution made, giving independence to the country.
Third General Elections won by the C.P.P. Constitutional disputes.
Date of Independence announced on September 18th.

1957: Constitutional disputes resolved. New Constitution came into effect, and Gold Coast became an independent nation within the British Commonwealth on March 6th, under the name 'Ghana'.
Sir Charles Arden-Clarke, the last British Governor of the country and its first Governor-General, left and replaced by Earl of Listowel.
Nkrumah attended British Commonwealth Prime Ministers' Conference in London.

BIBLIOGRAPHY

An attempt has been made to list below the books and reports which deal with aspects of the progress of events in Ghana as covered in this book. The list is by no means exhaustive.

A History of the Gold Coast, by W. E. F. Ward. (Allen & Unwin, London.) Covers the history of the country in general.

Modern Colonization, by Harrison Church. (Hutchinson's University Library, London.) Contains a detailed account of the Togoland problem.

The Position of the Chief in the Modern Political System of Ashanti, by K. A. Busia. (O.U.P., London.) An analysis of the power of the chief, his position and influence in Ashanti society.

The Gold Coast, by A. W. Cardinall. (Government Printer, Accra.) An account of the progress and development of the Gold Coast up to the late 1920s.

Freedom for the Gold Coast? by T. L. Hodgkin. (U.D.C. Pamphlet.) A brief analysis of the rise of the U.G.C.C. and the C.P.P.

West Africa, by F. J. Pedler. (Methuen, London.) Contains sections on the rise of the U.G.C.C. and its eclipse by the C.P.P. Includes a section on the Togoland problem.

The Gold Coast Revolution, by George Padmore. (Dobson, London.) Deals with the rise of Nkrumah and the C.P.P. up to about 1952.

Must We Lose Africa? by Colin Legum. (W. H. Allen, London.) Contains comments on Nkrumah's rise to power, and his attitude to the Volta River Project.

BIBLIOGRAPHY

Four Guineas, by Elspeth Huxley. (Chatto & Windus, London.) Reviews the Nkrumah Government during its first years in a section on Ghana.

The Machinery of Self-Government, by David Kimble. (Penguin, London.) Contains an excellent account of the Ghana Civil Service, Legislative Assembly and the organisation of public opinion.

Inside Africa, by John Gunther. (Hamish Hamilton, London.) Sections on Ghana deal with the economic and political progress of the country and the problems facing it and gives the life-history of Dr. Nkrumah.

The Heart of Africa, by Alexander Campbell. (Longmans Green, London.) The rise of the C.P.P. and Dr. Nkrumah are briefly dealt with, together with a personal assessment of Dr. Nkrumah.

The Gold Coast Legislative Council, by Martin Wight. An exhaustive study.

Kwame Nkrumah: His Rise to Power, by Bankole Timothy. (Allen & Unwin, London.) Undoubtedly the best account to date. Contains a brief assessment of the man.

Gold Coast to Ghana, by Paul Redmayne. (John Murray, London.) A lavishly illustrated account of the progress of the country between the years 1950 and 1956.

Africa Emergent, by W. H. Macmillan. (Penguin, London.) A survey of social, political and economic trends in British Africa.

The Gold Coast: A Survey of the Gold Coast and British Togoland, 1919-1946, by F. M. Bourret. (O.U.P., London.) A standard work on the country for the period it covers.

Ghana, autobiography of Kwame Nkrumah. (Nelson, Edinburgh.) The human story of the rise to power of the son of a goldsmith from an obscure corner of Ghana to world fame. Covers the political events of the country from about 1947 to 1956.

BIBLIOGRAPHY

Introduction to the History of West Africa, by J. D. Fage. (O.U.P., London.) Contains sections on the ancient and modern history of Ghana.

The New West Africa. (Allen & Unwin, London.) A symposium on the political and economic progress of the West African territories during recent years.

Ghana: A Brief Political and Economic Survey. (Information Department of the Royal Institute of International Affairs, London.) Certainly the best and fullest account to date of the evolution of Ghana within the last decade. Covers in detail the political and economic progress of the country, and contains reviews of Ghana's history and social structure.

The following official reports and publications may also be consulted:

Colonial Reports, Gold Coast, 1954.

Report of the Commission of Enquiry into Disturbances on the Gold Coast, 1948.

Gold Coast: Report to His Excellency the Governor by Committee on Constitutional Reform, 1949.

The Government's Proposals for Constitutional Reform, 1953.

Report of the Achimota Conference, 1956.

Government Report on the Achimota Conference, 1956.

Proposed Constitution of Ghana, February 1957.

In addition to the above works and reports, the following journals frequently contain interesting articles on Ghana: *African World, African Affairs, West Africa, West African Review, Africa* and *The New Commonwealth.*

A Stimulating Book on the Great Problems of Our Time

VISCOUNT SAMUEL

Belief and Action

An important book, in which this eminent British statesman surveys the greatest problems of our time and points a way out from the anxiety and insecurity and doubt in which we live. During the last few years Lord Samuel has established himself as a broadcaster of outstanding popularity, and millions of people have listened to his wise comments on current topics. "I hope," says Lord Samuel in the Introduction which he has written specially for this revised PAN edition, "that there is not one sentence which cannot be readily understood by anyone." Those who have heard his frequent broadcasts will know how clearly he expresses his ideas. Here are chapters on the world around us, on the present position of science and religion, on the fact of evil, on right and wrong, on the family, on poverty and property, on liberty, on 'The Nation and the World'; and there is an entirely new chapter on international affairs entitled 'The Present Situation'. Finally, Lord Samuel sums up the message of the whole book and suggests the kind of action that could be taken in order that we may emerge from the mental mists that now confuse us. (2/–)

"This man speaks as a doctor of the soul, as one who has deep insight into the problems, possibilities, and goals of development of the human race, and who has the prejudices and sorrows of the present generation clearly before his eyes."—The late PROFESSOR EINSTEIN.

"A profoundly interesting, helpful and stimulating book . . . wonderful value for money . . . It is a masterly survey of a vast field."—GERALD BULLETT in BBC broadcast.

"Lord Samuel tackles the problem of what a man can think and believe in this time of doubt and perplexity and indecision. . . . His book is full of wisdom and confidence, not of any easy faith but of faith in the future of man."—*John o' London's Weekly.*

How to Speak Clearly and Attractively

Mrs. A. M. HENDERSON

Good Speaking

To be able to speak well is not a gift granted to the few, the author points out in her Introduction: it is an achievement which is within the grasp of anyone who is prepared to work for it. This book, specially written for PAN by an author with a lifetime of experience, provides a course of study which sets aside much of the technicality usually involved in speech training, and concentrates instead on the development of the alliance between mind and voice which is so essential. The first part of the book is concerned with the practical aspects of good speaking, with chapters on Breathing, Articulation, Vowels, Accent, Inflexion and Modulation. The second part deals with a more elusive quality, that *something*—call it *personality* —which causes a voice to arrest and hold the attention; and here the author claims that her methods have more to offer than could be gained from a purely technical approach. Finally, Mrs. Henderson deals with the *use* of good speaking, and gives advice to all who want to read or speak in public, either for business or for pleasure. Throughout she makes her points clearly and informally, and she quotes passages of verse and prose which can be used by students. *2nd (revised) Edition.* (2/-)

"An eloquently written and well-planned book . . . that reflects the long practical experience the author has had in this field. There is an absence of technical terms, and the reader is led from one step to the next with ease, while the examples chosen for exercise and study are all of good quality."—*Drama*.

"Should be in the pocket of every amateur player."—*Amateur Stage*.

"This book should prove helpful to adults who seek introduction to an imaginative use of speech."—*Times Educational Supplement*.

"This delightful and profitable book. . . . I hope it will put many of the young in the way of right-doing in an important and civilising art."—SIR HECTOR HETHERINGTON, Principal and Vice-Chancellor of Glasgow University.

How to Write Clearly and Attractively

JOHN C. TARR

Good Handwriting

Many of us would like to improve our handwriting. But how? John C. Tarr in this book, which has been revised and considerably enlarged for this PAN edition, contends that the ideal model is a beautiful script similar in many ways to printed italic letters and quite unlike the Round Hand or Copperplate style which has for so long been admired and advocated in Europe. It is called the Chancery Script, and it can be acquired after a few hours' practice. Easy to learn, it is far less subject to deterioration than is Copperplate, and, once mastered, does not involve any sacrifice either of speed or character. Thus the reader who decides to follow Mr Tarr may be assured that he has achieved a permanent asset. *Bad* handwriting, as we all know, is a widespread nuisance in business and in private correspondence; it is, in fact, an insult to the recipient. "We should not speak in such a slovenly way," says Mr. Tarr, "nor dress as untidily, nor entertain friends so casually. Why, then, write to them in such a fashion?" How attractive, yet individualistic, the Chancery Script is may be seen from the examples of contemporary writing among the 78 line illustrations. Mr. Tarr also includes chapters on pens and nibs, on the historical development of written letters, and on early italic printing types. (2/–)

"Has an excellence of its own, and if I wanted to introduce someone to this subject, I would introduce him to this book."—*New Statesman*.

"A book likely to cause your child to reach for his pen and experiment."—*Parents' Review*.

Printed in the United States
35466LVS00001B/39